Measurements

Millimetres	Inches	Millimetres	Inches
2mm	1/16in	13cm	
3mm	1/8in	13.5cm	
4mm	1/6in	15cm	6in
5mm	1/4in	16cm	6½in
1cm	1/2in	18cm	7in
2cm	3/4in	19cm	7½in
2.5cm	1in	20cm	8in
3cm	1¼in	23cm	9in
4cm	1½in	24cm	9½in
4.5cm	1¾in	25.5cm	10in
5cm	2in	28cm	11in
6cm	2½in	30cm	12in
7.5cm	3in	32.5cm	13in
9cm	3½in	35cm	14in
10cm	4in	37.5cm	15in

Oven temperatures

	Fan	Gas
110°C	90°C	–
120°C	100°C	½
140°C	120°C	1
150°C	130°C	2
160°C	140°C	3
180°C	160°C	4
190°C	170°C	5
200°C	180°C	6
220°C	200°C	7
230°C	210°C	8
240°C	220°C	9

Sainsbury's
Cookbook
VOLUME ONE

Sainsbury's Cookbook

VOLUME ONE

Welcome...

...to the latest cookbook from Sainsbury's created especially for you. We have compiled recipes from the UK and from around the world, to give you ideas for cooking every day.

All the delicious dishes can be made from readily available ingredients and feature easy-to-follow step-by-step instructions, for great results every time, whatever your cooking ability.

The recipes are divided into clear sections, from Starters and light bites through to Fish and seafood and all types of Meat dishes, with a section devoted to Vegetarian recipes. The collection finishes off with Desserts followed closely by Cakes and bakes. So, it is easy to find inspiration for everyday cooking for your family or your friends.

Preparation and cooking times are given for each recipe, as well as nutritional information. The index at the back of the book will help you to find the right recipe fast.

We've used these icons to make everything clear at a glance

 Suitable for vegetarians

 Recipes containing 1 or more of your 5-a-day, to help you plan for healthier eating. Try to eat at least 5 different portions of fruit and veg a day. Fresh, frozen, dried, canned and juice all count.

Contents

Starters and light bites

Quick tuna pâté

This simple pâté - that uses mostly storecupboard staples - can be ready in minutes

50g unsalted butter
2 x 200g tins tuna in spring water by Sainsbury's, drained
1 tbsp olive oil
finely grated zest and juice of 1/2 lemon
2 tbsp chopped flat-leaf parsley leaves
25g fresh white breadcrumbs

TO SERVE
4 carrots, peeled and cut into batons
4 sticks of celery, washed and cut into batons
4 slices of soft white farmhouse bread by Sainsbury's, toasted

1 Place the butter in a small microwave-proof jug and heat it in a microwave on a medium heat for 30 seconds to 1 minute, or until melted. (Or melt it in a small saucepan over a very gentle heat, if you prefer.)

2 Put the tuna and melted butter along with the oil in a food processor and whizz until smooth. Add the lemon zest and juice, parsley and breadcrumbs. Season to taste, and pulse-blend to combine.

3 Spoon the pâté into four 150ml ramekins, cover and chill until ready to serve. Serve with crunchy vegetable crudités and toast.

Per serving: 1589kJ/379kcal (11%), 14.7g fat (21%), 6.9g saturates (35%), 10.4g sugars (12%), 1.27g salt (21%)

Why not try?
Substitute tinned mackerel (3 x 125g tins in oil, drained) for the tuna for a different fish taste and add a tablespoon or so of half-fat crème fraîche to help achieve the right consistency and a dash of mustard to help cut through the richness, if you feel that's necessary.

Cheese and paprika straws

These moreish pastry spirals, with the added note of smoky paprika, are ideal to serve with dips

100g unsalted butter
125g plain flour, sifted,
plus extra for dusting
1 egg yolk

1 tsp smoked paprika
by Sainsbury's
100g finely grated
Red Leicester

1 Freeze the butter for 30 minutes, until semi-frozen. Dust a large grater with flour (to stop the butter sticking) and grate the butter into a large bowl. Rub in the flour with your fingers. Add 4-5 tablespoons of cold water and bring it together to form a dough. Wrap it in cling film and chill for 30 minutes. Preheat the oven to 200°C/180°C fan/gas 6.

2 Roll the pastry out on to a lightly floured work surface so that it makes a rectangle of pastry about 20cm x 30cm.

3 Brush the surface of the pastry with the egg yolk and sprinkle over the smoked paprika. Sprinkle the cheese over in a thin layer, and press it in well with the flat of your hands. Fold the pastry in half and press down well to enclose the cheese totally.

4 Next, cut the pastry into 15 strips, each about 1cm wide. Hold the top of each strip and gently twist the bottom a few times to create the spiral of the pastry straws.

5 Place the cheese straws onto a baking sheet and bake for 15 minutes at the top of the oven. Cool on the tray for 5 minutes, then transfer to a wire rack to cool completely.

Per serving: 464kJ/112kcal (6%), 8.2g fat (12%), 4.8g saturates (24%), <0.5g sugars (<1%), 0.12g salt (2%)

Cook's tip
The cheese straws can be frozen, spaced well apart on a tray at the end of step 4, then transferred to a freezer bag and kept for up to 12 weeks. Defrost thoroughly in the fridge and bake as in step 5.

Trio of dips

Each dip offers different flavour combinations. Serve with crudités

ROASTED RED PEPPER, FETA AND MINT DIP
MAKES 18 portions
3 red peppers, quartered and deseeded
200g feta cheese
200g light soft cheese by Sainsbury's
1 garlic clove, chopped
3 tbsp finely chopped mint leaves
2 tbsp olive oil
1 tbsp lemon juice

AVOCADO LIME CREAM DIP
MAKES 12 portions
2 medium avocados
4 spring onions, chopped
2 green chillies, deseeded and finely chopped
15g fresh coriander
juice of 2 limes
1 tbsp olive oil
150ml soured cream by Sainsbury's

CURRY SPICED YOGURT, CORIANDER AND MANGO CHUTNEY DIP
MAKES 13 portions
6 tbsp mango chutney
15g fresh coriander, chopped
4 spring onions, chopped
juice of 2 limes
175g light soft cheese by Sainsbury's
250g Greek-style yogurt
1/2 tsp curry powder
1/4 tsp turmeric
hot pepper sauce, to taste

Roasted red pepper, feta and mint dip

1 Grill and peel the pepper quarters. Place the peppers, along with the rest of the ingredients in a food processor or blender; pulse until well blended but still retaining some texture.

2 If necessary, adjust the consistency by gradually adding water 1 tablespoon at a time. Season to taste.

3 Cover and refrigerate for 30 minutes to allow the flavours to mingle. Serve chilled with crunchy vegetable crudités.

Per portion: 283kJ/68kcal (3.6%), 5.0g fat (7%), 2.9g saturates (15%), 2.0g sugars (2%), 0.25g salt (4%)

Avocado lime cream dip

1 Place the avocados, spring onions, chillies, coriander, lime juice, olive oil and soured cream in a food processor or blender; pulse until smooth. Season to taste.

2 Cover and refrigerate for 15 minutes to allow the flavours to blend and deepen. Serve chilled with crunchy vegetable crudités.

Per portion: 341kJ/83kcal (4%), 8.1g fat (12%), 2.7g saturates (14%), 0.8g sugars (1%), 0.02g salt (<1%)

Curry spiced yogurt, coriander and mango chutney dip

1 Place all the ingredients except the hot pepper sauce in a food processor or blender; on the pulse setting, mix until well blended.

2 Season to taste and add a few drops of hot pepper sauce, depending on how hot you want the dip. Cover and chill for 30 minutes. Serve chilled with crunchy vegetable crudités.

Per portion: 284kJ/68kcal (3%), 3.4g fat (5%), 2.2g saturates (11%), 6.8g sugars (8%), 0.26g salt (4%)

SERVES 6
PREP 1¹/₂ hours, plus rising
COOK 10 minutes

Fatayer with herbs

These little flatbreads sprinkled with a blend of herbs are popular as street food in Lebanon, Syria and Jordan. Enjoy on their own as a snack or as an accompaniment to mezze dishes

7g fast action dried yeast
by Sainsbury's
¹/₂ tsp sugar
450g strong bread flour,
plus extra for dusting
¹/₂ tsp salt

2-3 tbsp olive oil,
plus extra for greasing
3-4 tbsp herb mix (use
dried thyme or oregano
with crushed dried chillies)

1 In a small bowl, dissolve the yeast and the sugar in a mixture of 4ml boiling water and 6ml cold water. Set the bowl aside for 10 minutes, or until frothy.

2 Sift the flour into another bowl along with the salt. Make a well in the centre and add the yeast mixture. Add 300ml of lukewarm water and draw the flour in from the sides and mix to form a dough.

3 Turn the dough out onto a floured surface and knead well for about 10 minutes, until it is smooth and elastic. Pour a drop of the oil into the base of the bowl, roll the dough in it and cover with a damp cloth or some cling film. Leave the dough in a warm place to rise for about 1 hour, until it has roughly doubled in size.

4 Preheat the oven to 200°C/180°C fan/gas 6, and lightly grease two baking trays.

5 In a small bowl, mix together the herb mix with the oil and bind it to a paste. Knock back the dough - transfer from the bowl to a work surface and knead it lightly to get rid of the excess air out of the dough. Divide the dough into about 20 parts. Knead each part into a ball, flatten and stretch it and smear it with some of the herb paste.

6 Place the flatbreads on the prepared baking trays and bake for about 10 minutes, until golden. Best served warm.

Per serving: 1299kJ/308kcal (15%), 6.1g fat (9%), 1.0g saturates (5%), 1.5g sugars (2%), 0.04g salt (1%)

Why not try?

For a different flavour of the Middle East, make your own zahtar and use the same quantity as for the herb mix above. For the zahtar, mix the following together and keep in an airtight container: 4 tsp sesame seeds; 4 tbsp finely chopped fresh oregano; 4 tsp dried marjoram; 4 tsp sumac; and 4 tsp ground cumin.

Chicken satay

Recreate the aromas of Malaysian street food at any
gathering with these super-tasty skewers

350g skinless, boneless chicken
breast, finely sliced
lime wedges, to serve

FOR THE MARINADE
1 stalk lemongrass, peeled of
hard layers, and finely chopped
2 spring onions, white part only,
roughly chopped
1 garlic clove, roughly chopped

2cm fresh root ginger, peeled
and roughly chopped
$\frac{1}{2}$ tsp turmeric
1 tbsp soft brown sugar
2 tbsp soy sauce
$\frac{1}{2}$ tbsp fish sauce
1 tbsp sunflower oil

FOR THE PEANUT SAUCE
1 tbsp sweet chilli sauce

1 tbsp soy sauce
1 tbsp fish sauce
1 tsp chilli flakes (optional)
juice of $\frac{1}{2}$ lime
150g crunchy peanut butter
by Sainsbury's
100ml coconut milk (you could
make this up using 25g creamed
coconut and 100ml boiling water
or use some of tinned version)

1 Whizz the marinade ingredients in a blender until you get the consistency of a paste.
Pour over the chicken and toss. Cover and leave in the fridge for 1 hour. Meanwhile, soak
8 bamboo skewers in water and preheat the grill for cooking.

2 Next, put all of the ingredients for the peanut sauce in a pan and stir over a gentle
heat until they melt into one. Transfer to a small bowl, to serve.

3 Thread the chicken onto the skewers, folding each piece of meat if necessary. Line the
grill tray with foil and grill the chicken for 4-5 minutes on each side, until crispy and cooked
through, with no pink remaining. Serve with the peanut sauce on the side and lime wedges.

Per serving: 1917kJ/459kcal (23%), 26.8g fat (38%), 7.7g saturates (39%), 12.6g sugars
(14%), 3.01g salt (50%)

Cook's tip
To avoid setting the bamboo skewers on fire when
you put the chicken under the grill or on the
barbecue, soak the wooden skewers in cold water
first for at least 20 minutes. Then, they'll be
ready to use.

SERVES 5
PREP 30 minutes
COOK 30 minutes

Spicy pepper empanadas

These little snacks are a favourite in South America where they are made with a range of sweet and savoury fillings

FOR THE FILLING
1 tbsp olive oil
1 large onion, sliced
1 red pepper, deseeded
and chopped
3 fresh red or green jalapeño
chillies by Sainsbury's, chopped

2 garlic cloves, finely chopped
2 tbsp dry sherry
300g cooked chickpeas, drained
2 tbsp finely chopped
coriander leaves
2 tbsp finely chopped flat-leaf
parsley leaves

FOR THE PASTRY
100g unsalted butter
juice of 1 lemon
225g plain flour, plus extra
for dusting
1 tsp paprika
sunflower oil, for frying

1 For the filling, heat the oil in a medium pan, add the onion and season to taste. Cook on a low heat for 2-3 minutes, until soft. Add the red pepper, jalapeños and garlic, and cook for 10 minutes, or until the pepper starts to soften. Add the sherry to the pan, increase the heat and cook for 2 minutes. Tip in the chickpeas, coriander and parsley and stir. Season to taste.

2 Transfer to a food processor and pulse the mixture to break it up, but do not mince it.

3 To make the pastry, melt the butter in a pan, add the lemon juice followed by 100ml water. Combine the flour and paprika in a bowl, add the melted butter and mix to a paste.

4 Knead gently for 2 minutes and then leave to rest for 2-3 minutes at room temperature.

5 To form the empanadas, roll the pastry out on a floured surface to about 3mm thick, adding more flour if needed. Cut out 10 rounds using a 10cm diameter cutter. Spoon a generous amount of filling onto one half of each round, wet around the edges with water, fold over and seal with a pinch.

6 Pour sunflower oil into a small, deep-sided frying pan, to a depth of 1cm and heat to medium. Add 3 empanadas at a time and cook for 2-3 minutes on each side until golden. Transfer to a plate lined with kitchen paper. Serve hot or warm.

Per serving: 2478kJ/595kcal (30%), 34.1g fat (56%), 12.7g saturates (64%), 4.6g sugars (5%), 0.07g salt (1%)

Cook's tip
Roast the leftover chickpeas for a great savoury nibble. Toss in a little olive oil and a favourite spice mix, spread out on a baking tray and bake for 30 minutes at 200°C/180°C fan/gas 6.

Mexican prawn bites

These crunchy Mexican-style nibbles are perfect washed down with a cold beer or a chilled lime juice and mint spritzer

4-6 tortillas
2 tbsp vegetable oil
1-2 tbsp chipotle chilli
paste by Sainsbury's
350g frozen large peeled prawns
by Sainsbury's, defrosted

2 tomatoes, finely chopped
1 tbsp finely chopped
red onion
juice of ½ lime
a handful of fresh
coriander, chopped

FOR THE GUACAMOLE
1 small ripe avocado,
lightly mashed

1 Preheat the oven to 190°C/170°C fan/gas 5. Next, use a 6cm cookie cutter to stamp out circles from the tortillas. Alternatively, use a sharp knife to cut around a small cup to make the circles. Brush the discs all over with a little of the vegetable oil and place on a baking sheet. Bake in a preheated oven for 5-7 minutes, until just crisp. Then, remove from the oven, cover and set aside to cool.

2 Mix together the remaining oil with the chipotle paste and then stir through the prawns. Heat a non-stick pan over a high heat and cook the prawns for 3-5 minutes, turning halfway, until lightly golden and cooked through.

3 In a bowl, mix the mashed avocado with the tomatoes, onion, lime juice and most of the chopped coriander leaves, and then season the guacamole to taste.

4 Arrange the tortillas on a serving platter and top each with a dot of guacamole and then a prawn. Finish with a scattering of the remaining coriander.

Per serving: 1991kJ/ 475kcal (24%), 18.2g fat (26%), 4.6g saturates (23%), 5.9g sugars (7%), 2.6g salt (43%)

Did you know?
Chipotle paste is a fiery smoky sauce used in lots of Mexican recipes. It's made from dried jalapeño chillies that are smoked and then mixed with a spicy sauce. It's pretty hot, so use sparingly, adding 1 teaspoon to pep up a chilli con carne or rubbing a little over chicken drumsticks for a spicy barbecue dish.

MAKES 12
PREP 20 minutes
COOK 10 minutes

Courgette fritters with yogurt dip

Transport yourself to Greece with these delicate fritters that make a perfect starter or light lunch

200g small courgettes, coarsely grated
100g ricotta cheese by Sainsbury's
1 large egg
2 tbsp plain flour
2 garlic cloves, crushed
a small handful of fresh basil leaves, chopped
a small handful of fresh flat-leaf parsley leaves, chopped
light olive oil, for frying

FOR THE YOGURT DIP
½ garlic clove, crushed
2 tbsp finely chopped dill fronds
200g Greek-style yogurt
juice of ½ lemon

1 Squeeze the grated courgettes dry in a clean tea towel.

2 In a bowl, whisk together the ricotta cheese, egg and flour. Add the crushed garlic, the chopped herbs and season well. Next, mix in the courgettes.

3 To make the dip, mix the garlic with the dill and yogurt, followed by a squeeze of lemon juice, then season to taste. Cover and set aside in a bowl.

4 Fill a frying pan with oil to a depth of 1cm and fry tablespoonfuls of the courgette batter over a medium heat for 2-3 minutes on each side, until golden. Drain on kitchen paper and serve hot with the yogurt on the side.

Per serving: 485kJ/117kcal (6%), 10.5g fat (15%), 2.8g saturates (14%), 1.5g sugars (2%), 0.07g salt (1%)

Did you know?

Salting grated flesh from larger courgettes, leaving them in a sieve for 1 hour to drain and then rinsing them offsets any wateriness; smaller ones won't need salting.

MAKES 20
PREP 10 minutes
COOK 30 minutes

Baby baked potatoes with soured cream

Serve these bite-sized potatoes as a canapé or starter for guests. Experiment with other herbs – snipped chives on top work well, too

20 tiny new potatoes, pricked
1 tbsp olive oil
125ml soured cream
by Sainsbury's

sprigs of fresh dill and freshly
ground black pepper, to serve

1 Preheat the oven to 200°C/180°C fan/gas 6.

2 Toss the potatoes with the oil until they are evenly coated. Place on a baking sheet and cook in a preheated oven for 30 minutes, or until soft on the inside and crisp on the outside.

3 Cool completely. Cut a cross on the top of each potato and squeeze gently at the base to open each one up slightly. Top each baby potato with 1 teaspoon of soured cream followed by the dill and black pepper. Serve at once.

Per serving: 163kJ/39kcal (2%), 1.7g fat (2%), 0.8g saturates (4%), 0.5g sugars (1%), <0.01g salt (<1%)

Get ahead
Bake the potatoes a day in advance and store in an airtight container in the fridge. Crisp up in a preheated oven (200°C/180°C fan/gas 6) for 5 minutes and top with the soured cream just before serving.

Chicken rolls

Sausage rolls are a family favourite, but try this chicken alternative for something a little lighter-tasting

2 large skinless,
boneless chicken breasts
1 small garlic clove, blanched
and crushed
a handful of fresh parsley
leaves, chopped

375g ready-rolled puff
pastry by Sainsbury's
plain flour, for dusting
1 egg yolk

1 Preheat the oven to 200°C/180°C fan/gas 6. Next, place the chicken and garlic in a blender and whizz until smooth. Then, pulse or stir in the parsley leaves until just combined and add seasoning, to taste.

2 Unroll the pastry onto a lightly floured work surface. Cut in half lengthways. Place half the chicken mixture along the middle of each pastry strip. Then, brush along the long edges with the egg yolk. Tightly roll up the pastry around the chicken to form a long tube, pinching the edge to seal. Then, use a sharp knife to cut each roll into 5 pieces and place on a baking sheet. Brush over the top with more egg.

3 Cook in a preheated oven for 20-25 minutes, until the pastry is puffed and golden and the chicken is cooked through, with no pink remaining.

Per serving: 858kJ/205kcal (10%), 10.6g fat (15%), 5.0g saturates (25%), 0.6g sugars (1%), 0.21g salt (4%)

MAKES 20
PREP 20 minutes,
plus chilling
COOK 10 minutes

Thai salmon bites

These versatile fish cakes cover all the bases – make them bite-sized for canapés, larger for a starter or eat with rice noodles for an aromatic main course

500g salmon fillet
115g green beans, trimmed and finely chopped
1 green or red chilli, deseeded and very finely chopped
finely grated zest of 1 lime
1 tsp lemongrass paste by Sainsbury's

1 tbsp fish sauce
1 tbsp finely snipped chives
1 egg white, lightly beaten
plain flour, for dusting
vegetable oil, for deep-frying
lime wedges, to serve

1 Flake the salmon into a bowl, picking it over carefully to remove any small bones. Mix in the green beans, chilli, lime zest, lemongrass paste, fish sauce and chives. Then, add the egg white, stirring to bind the mixture together.

2 Next, dust your hands with flour and shape the mixture into 20 small balls. Flatten them slightly into round cakes, place on a plate or board, spaced slightly apart (so they don't stick together), cover and chill for 1 hour, or until firm.

3 Heat the oil to 160°C in a large pan or deep-fat fryer. Dust the cakes with flour and deep-fry them for 3 minutes, or until golden and cooked through, in batches. Drain on a plate lined with kitchen paper and serve with lemon wedges.

Per serving: 397kJ/96kcal (5%), 7.8g fat (11%), 1.2g saturates (6%), <0.5g sugars (<1%), 0.24g salt (4%)

Get ahead
Make these fish cakes the day before, cover and chill – the flavours will deepen. Return them to room temperature before picking up the recipe at step 3.

Salads

Grilled chicken Caesar salad

This favourite salad is a perfect combination of succulent chicken, crunchy croutons and crisp lettuce all brought together with a quick-to-make update on the classic Caesar dressing

100g day-old baguette or other rustic white bread, trimmed of crusts and cut into 2cm cubes

4 tbsp olive oil

400g skinless, boneless chicken breasts

1 large Romaine lettuce heart, leaves broken into bite-sized pieces

30g Parmesan cheese shavings, to serve

FOR THE DRESSING

100ml extra virgin olive oil

1 tbsp Dijon mustard

3 tbsp reduced-fat mayonnaise by Sainsbury's

4 anchovy fillets, chopped

1/2 tsp Worcestershire sauce

1 garlic clove, crushed

2 tbsp finely grated Parmesan cheese

a pinch of caster sugar

1 Preheat the oven to 200°C/180°C fan/gas 6. To make the croutons, toss the bread cubes with 3 tablespoons of the olive oil, season to taste and spread them out on a large baking sheet, in a single layer if possible. Cook them at the top of the oven for 6–8 minutes, turning occasionally, until they are golden on all sides. Watch carefully, so that they do not burn. Cover with a clean tea towel and set aside to cool.

2 If you do not have a griddle pan, preheat the grill on its highest setting. Meanwhile, rub the chicken breasts with the remaining olive oil, season to taste and cook either on the griddle pan or under the hot grill for 5 minutes on each side, or until cooked through, with no pink remaining. Cover and set aside to cool, then slice.

3 To make the dressing, put all the ingredients into the bowl of a mini food processor, or into a suitable container for a hand blender, and process or blend until they have emulsified into a thick, creamy dressing. Season to taste.

4 To serve, put the lettuce in a large bowl and toss it in the dressing. Scatter the croutons and Parmesan shavings over and arrange the warm chicken slices on top.

Per serving: 2512kJ/604kcal (30%), 42.8g fat (61%), 7.9g saturates (40%), 2.0g sugars (2%), 1.71g salt (29%)

Antipasti salad

Combine all the usual salty and sweet flavours of traditional antipasti in this delicious and vibrant salad

400g French beans, trimmed
3 tbsp chopped parsley
2 tsp fresh lemon thyme leaves
1 tbsp chopped fennel fronds
2 tbsp extra virgin olive oil
1 x 120g bag of bistro salad
by Sainsbury's
4 slices Parma ham,
thinly shredded

400g tin artichoke hearts by
Sainsbury's, drained and
hearts cut in half
16 black olives, pitted and chopped
125g cherry tomatoes, halved
2 spring onions, chopped
3 tbsp chopped chervil

FOR THE DRESSING
5 tbsp extra virgin olive oil
1/2 garlic clove, crushed
1/2 tbsp balsamic vinegar

1 Blanch the French beans in a pan of boiling water for 5-7 minutes. Then refresh under cold running water and drain.

2 Place the beans in a wide, shallow salad bowl. Season to taste and scatter over half the parsley, lemon thyme and fennel. Drizzle over the olive oil, toss and set aside.

3 Make the dressing by pouring the olive oil into a small jug. Whisk in the garlic and balsamic vinegar and season to taste.

4 Scatter the salad leaves over the beans, followed by the ham, prepared artichoke hearts, olives, tomatoes and spring onions. Whisk the dressing again and drizzle it over the salad. Toss, sprinkle over the chervil and serve straightaway.

Per serving: 1264kJ/305kcal (15%), 23.5g fat (34%), 4.2g saturates (21%), 5.8g sugars (6%), 1.37g salt (23%)

Apricot, pine nut and coriander couscous

This Middle Eastern-inspired salad works equally well whether served as a light lunch or as a partner to a slow-cooked lamb dish, such as stifado (see p180)

300g couscous by Sainsbury's
1½ tbsp olive oil
1 tbsp powdered vegetable stock (bouillon)
50g pine nuts
100g dried apricots, finely chopped
a large handful of fresh coriander, finely chopped
4½ tbsp extra virgin olive oil
juice of 1 large lemon

1 Boil a kettle of water. Pour the couscous into a bowl and drizzle over the olive oil. Stir through the couscous, scatter over the powdered vegetable stock and mix it in.

2 Pour 525ml boiling water over the couscous and stir briefly. The water should just cover the grains. Immediately cover the bowl with cling film or a clean tea towel.

3 Leave for 5 minutes, then test the grains, which should be nearly soft; check that all the water has been absorbed. Fork over the couscous and leave it to cool, forking it occasionally to stop it from sticking in clumps and keeping the grains separate.

4 Meanwhile, dry-fry the pine nuts in a non-stick frying pan over a medium heat, stirring, until they brown; take care as they can burn quickly. Set aside to cool.

5 In a large serving bowl, toss together the cooled couscous, pine nuts, apricots and coriander. Mix in the oil and lemon juice and season to taste. Serve straightaway.

Per serving: 1251kJ/299kcal (15%), 16.5g fat (24%), 2.0g saturates (10%), 6.5g sugars (7%), 0.74g salt (12%)

Why not try?
Use pomegranate seeds for a piquant, ruby-tinged salad.

Herbs

< **Mint** is an aromatic herb and the one most commonly used for cooking is spearmint. Its versatility ranges from dishes of lamb to new potatoes, peas and other summer vegetables.

> **Coriander** leaves have a bittersweet, fresh citrus taste and make an ideal flavour enhancer. They lose a little flavour when cooked, so it's best to add towards the end of cooking.

< **Thyme** (common and lemon) is a versatile herb. It enhances roast vegetables, poultry and fish. It dries well too.

> **Dill** fronds have a fresh aniseed flavour. Pair it with fish, rice, salad and yogurt.

^ **Bay leaves** have a bittersweet spicy taste and are an essential ingredient in bouquet garni. Great in stews and soups. Dried bay leaves make an invaluable store cupboard herb as they keep their flavour when dried.

> **Rosemary** is strongly aromatic with a clean, woody flavour. It's a perfect partner to lamb, pies and baking. Use sparingly, though, as it can overpower easily.

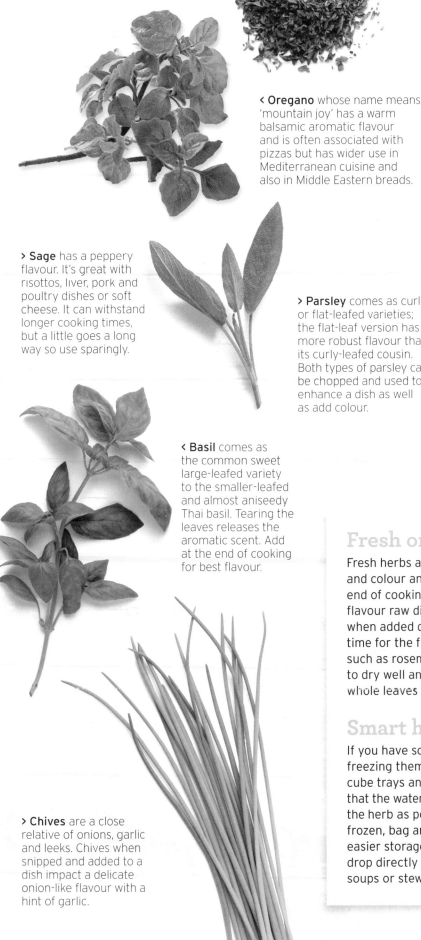

< Oregano whose name means 'mountain joy' has a warm balsamic aromatic flavour and is often associated with pizzas but has wider use in Mediterranean cuisine and also in Middle Eastern breads.

> Sage has a peppery flavour. It's great with risottos, liver, pork and poultry dishes or soft cheese. It can withstand longer cooking times, but a little goes a long way so use sparingly.

> Parsley comes as curly or flat-leafed varieties; the flat-leaf version has a more robust flavour than its curly-leafed cousin. Both types of parsley can be chopped and used to enhance a dish as well as add colour.

< Basil comes as the common sweet large-leafed variety to the smaller-leafed and almost aniseedy Thai basil. Tearing the leaves releases the aromatic scent. Add at the end of cooking for best flavour.

> Chives are a close relative of onions, garlic and leeks. Chives when snipped and added to a dish impact a delicate onion-like flavour with a hint of garlic.

Fresh or dried?

Fresh herbs add a certain vibrancy of flavour and colour and are best added towards the end of cooking time, used as a garnish or to flavour raw dishes. Dried herbs work well when added during cooking, so that there's time for the flavours to infuse. Woody herbs, such as rosemary, oregano and thyme, tend to dry well and maintain their flavour, as do whole leaves such as bay or curry leaves.

Smart herb use

If you have some left over fresh herbs, try freezing them. Chop them up, place in ice cube trays and cover with water, ensuring that the water covers as much of the herb as possible. Once frozen, bag and label for easier storage. To use, drop directly into soups or stews.

Roasted beetroot, goat's cheese and walnut salad

The pairing of earthy roasted beetroots with tangy goat's cheese makes a refreshing lunch or starter

6 small raw beetroots, peeled
and quartered
2 tbsp olive oil
75g walnut halves
1 x 170g bag of Italian-style
salad by Sainsbury's
100g French goat's cheese
Taste the Difference, crumbled

FOR THE DRESSING
4 tbsp extra virgin olive oil
2 tbsp cider vinegar
1 tsp Dijon mustard
1 tsp runny honey

1 Preheat the oven to 200°C/180°C fan/gas 6. Turn the beetroots through the oil and spread out on a large baking sheet. Bake in a preheated oven for 30–35 minutes, turning occasionally, until tender and colouring slightly at the edges. Remove from the oven, cover and set aside to cool.

2 Meanwhile, toast the walnuts in a dry frying pan on a medium heat until they start to colour slightly at the edges, but do not burn. Take them off the heat, cool then roughly chop.

3 In a large salad bowl, whisk together the ingredients for the dressing and season to taste.

4 When the beetroots have cooled, toss the salad leaves through the dressing. Gently mix in the beetroots and walnuts and crumble the goat's cheese over the top to serve.

Per serving: 1746kJ/426kcal (21%), 35.6g fat (51%), 7.5g saturates (38%), 12.6g sugars (14%), 0.71g salt (12%)

Chicken noodle salad

All the elements of this vibrant Asian-inspired salad can be made ahead, making it a quick-to-throw-together midweek meal

300g fresh rice noodles
by Sainsbury's
4 tbsp crunchy peanut butter
1 tbsp soy sauce
1-2 tbsp sweet chilli sauce
2 ready-cooked chicken breasts
$^{1}/_{2}$ cucumber, sliced
1 spring onion, sliced

TO SERVE
a handful of fresh coriander leaves
lime wedges

1 Prepare the noodles following the pack instructions. Then, place the cooked noodles in a sieve over the sink and refresh with cold running water until cool then drain.

2 Stir together the peanut butter, soy and sweet chilli sauces with 3-4 tablespoons of boiling water until smooth.

3 Remove any skin and bones from the chicken and then, using a fork, tear it into shreds.

4 In a large bowl, toss together the cooked noodles with the chicken, cucumber, spring onion and half of the sauce. Arrange on serving plates, spoon over the remaining sauce then scatter over the coriander and serve with lime wedges.

Per serving: 1267kJ/302kcal (15%), 12.5g fat (18%), 2.4g saturates (12%), 7.7g sugars (9%), 1.19g salt (20%)

Love your leftovers
Pep up leftover roast chicken by using it in this Asian-style noodle salad.

Panzanella

History has it that Tuscan farmers used to take this delectable bread salad with them to eat in the fields. Panzanella (from the Italian 'pan' for bread and 'zanella' for basket) means that good-quality bread, even when it is past its best, is never wasted

350g unsliced, stale, dense-textured white bread, such as ciabatta or sourdough, roughly torn into bite-sized pieces
600g mixed tomatoes (different colours and sizes), at room temperature, all roughly chopped into bite-sized chunks

1 red onion, finely chopped
2 garlic cloves, finely chopped
2 tbsp cappucine capers by Sainsbury's in brine, drained
a bunch of fresh basil, leaves roughly torn

FOR THE DRESSING
6 tbsp extra virgin olive oil
3 tbsp red wine vinegar
½ tsp mustard powder
½ tsp caster sugar

1 Place the bread, tomatoes, onion, garlic and capers in a large serving bowl. Season to taste and stir well to combine.

2 Place the dressing ingredients in a small jug, season to taste and stir well. Pour over the bread and tomato mixture and gently toss in the dressing to coat.

3 Cover and set aside for at least 10 minutes and up to 2 hours, at room temperature, to allow the flavours to mingle. Stir the basil leaves into the salad just before serving.

Per serving: 1173kJ/280kcal (14%), 12.9g fat (18%), 1.8g saturates (9%), 6.6g sugars (7%), 0.91g salt (15%)

Why not try?
Add some pitted black olives and drained anchovies for a salad with more robust and piquant flavours.

Quinoa salad with mango, lime and toasted coconut

Growing in popularity, quinoa is a great alternative to wheat-containing grains such as couscous

50g desiccated or flaked coconut
300g quinoa
410g tin butter beans by Sainsbury's, drained and rinsed
½ red onion, finely chopped
1 large mango, peeled, stoned and cut into bite-sized pieces

1 lime, peeled, segmented and segments halved
a handful of fresh mint, finely chopped
a handful of fresh flat-leaf parsley, finely chopped

FOR THE DRESSING
3 tbsp olive oil
1 tbsp white wine vinegar
a pinch of sugar

1 Toast the coconut by dry-frying it in a pan over a medium heat for 2–3 minutes, until golden, stirring so that it doesn't burn. Remove from the heat, cover and allow to cool.

2 To make the dressing, place all the ingredients in a small bowl or jug and whisk. Taste and adjust the seasoning as needed.

3 Cook the quinoa according to the pack instructions. Drain well and tip into a large serving bowl. While the quinoa is still warm, stir through the butter beans, onion, mango, lime, mint and parsley, and season to taste.

4 Pour over the dressing and stir through. Finish off with a sprinkling of the toasted coconut on top and serve immediately.

Per serving: 1979kJ/472kcal (24%), 19.5g fat (28%), 8.3g saturates (42%), 10.8g sugars (12%), 0.12g salt (2%)

Fish and seafood

SERVES 4
PREP 15 minutes
COOK 6-10 minutes

Lemon shallot crab cakes

Fresh crabs from the Chesapeake Bay are traditionally used to make these famous Maryland crab cakes, but salmon works well too

300g cooked white and
brown crabmeat
1 egg
100g crushed crackers or
dried breadcrumbs
juice of 1 lemon, plus extra
to serve
finely grated zest of 2 lemons
1 shallot, finely chopped
2 garlic cloves, crushed
peanut or sunflower oil,
for frying

FOR THE AÏOLI
220g reduced-fat mayonnaise
by Sainsbury's
juice of 1 lemon
a bunch of spring onions,
sliced
2 garlic cloves, crushed

1 Rinse and pick over the crabmeat, being careful to remove any pieces of shell, then drain well. In a bowl, mix together the crab, egg, crackers, lemon juice and zest. Add the shallot and garlic and mix well.

2 Take a quarter of the mixture and form a cake 7.5cm in diameter, cover and set aside on a plate. Repeat to make 3 more cakes.

3 Pour the oil into a large, heavy-based frying pan to a depth of at least 2.5cm. Heat the oil to 190°C and fry the cakes for 3-5 minutes on each side or until golden.

4 Meanwhile, make the aïoli. Mix together the mayonnaise, lemon juice, spring onions and garlic in a bowl and season to taste. Serve these crab cakes hot with the aïoli on the side and an extra squeeze of lemon.

Per serving: 2398kJ/577kcal (29%), 43.1g fat (62%), 5.7g saturates (29%), 4.3g sugars (5%), 2.01g salt (34%)

Why not try?
Add a finely chopped jalapeño or other mild green chilli to step 1 for a spicy twist.

Mackerel teriyaki

This Japanese-style mackerel dish is a tasty way to enjoy this delicious and sustainable fish

2 garlic cloves, finely chopped
2cm piece of fresh root ginger, peeled and finely chopped
2 tbsp caster sugar
4 tbsp rice vinegar by Sainsbury's
4 tbsp mirin
4 tbsp sake
4 tbsp soy sauce
4 fresh mackerel fillets, about 100g each, from Sainbury's fish counter

1 tbsp vegetable oil
chopped spring onions, to garnish

TO SERVE
quick-to-cook noodles by Sainsbury's
Oriental vegetable stir fry by Sainsbury's

1 Place the garlic, ginger, sugar, vinegar, mirin, sake and soy sauce in a small pan and bring to the boil. Reduce the heat and simmer for about 10 minutes, until the mixture has thickened to a coating consistency.

2 Season the fish to taste on both sides. Heat the oil in a large, non-stick frying pan over a medium heat. Add the mackerel skin-side down and cook for 2 minutes until crisp.

3 Turn the fish over and cook for 1 minute, or until it is cooked through and the flesh is opaque and flakes easily. Add the sauce to the pan and cook for a further 2 minutes.

4 Place the mackerel on serving plates, drizzle with a little of the sauce and garnish with the spring onions. Serve with noodles and stir-fried vegetables, both cooked according to the pack instructions.

Per serving: 2304kJ/550kcal (28%), 25.8g fat (37%), 4.2g saturates (21%), 20.2g sugars (202%), 2.26g salt (38%)

Fried prawns with lemon aïoli

The flaky Japanese panko breadcrumb coating gives these prawns a wonderful crunch. Mix up a citrus mayo or an Asian-inspired dipping sauce for a flavour bonanza

500ml sunflower oil, for frying
1 egg
130g plain flour
1 tsp paprika
$^1/_2$ tsp cayenne pepper
75g panko or breadcrumbs from day-old bread
24 frozen raw peeled jumbo king prawns by Sainsbury's, defrosted
lemon wedges, to serve

FOR THE LEMON AÏOLI
110g reduced-fat mayonnaise by Sainsbury's
juice of $^1/_2$ lemon
3 spring onions, chopped
2 garlic cloves, crushed

1 In a large, heavy-based saucepan, or deep-fat fryer, heat the oil to 190°C.

2 Break the egg into a bowl, add 1 tablespoon of water and whisk with a fork. In a separate large bowl, mix the flour, paprika, cayenne pepper and breadcrumbs.

3 Dip the prawns in the egg wash and toss them in the breadcrumb mixture, coating each one evenly. Fry the prawns in batches of 6, as overcrowding can mean the prawns will not brown well, for 3–4 minutes each or until golden and cooked through.

4 For the aïoli, whisk the mayonnaise, lemon juice, spring onions and garlic in a small bowl and season to taste. Serve in a small bowl alongside the prawns with lemon wedges.

Per serving: 1995kJ/477kcal (24%), 26.2g fat (37%), 3.5g saturates (18%), 2.9g sugars (3%), 0.48g salt (8%)

Why not try?
For a baked version, add 75g grated Parmesan cheese to the breadcrumbs and bake the coated prawns at 230°C/210°C fan/gas 8 for 5–7 minutes, or until golden, turning once so they are evenly coloured and cooked through. If you prefer Asian flavours to aïoli then combine 2 tbsp runny honey, 2 tbsp soy sauce and $^1/_2$ tbsp ground ginger for a tangy dipping sauce.

Fish Kievs

Revive this retro dish with a twist. Let the garlic butter work its magic on the inside while the crust crisps up on the outside

40g unsalted butter, softened
1 garlic clove, crushed
a handful of fresh
parsley, chopped
4 thick, skinless, boneless white
fish fillets, from Sainsbury's
fish counter

2 tbsp sunflower oil, plus a little
for greasing
75g dried breadcrumbs
2 x 170g bags of Italian-style
salad by Sainsbury's, to serve

1 Preheat the oven to 220°C/200°C fan/gas 7. Mix together the butter, garlic and parsley until well combined.

2 Place the fish on a chopping board and, using a small, sharp knife, make a little pocket in the centre of each fillet. Gently push a spoonful of butter inside each pocket then use your fingers to smooth over the gap in the fish.

3 Liberally brush most of the oil all over the fish until well covered and season to taste.

4 Pour the breadcrumbs onto a plate and turn the fish over until well coated. Then transfer the fish to a lightly oiled, shallow baking tray and drizzle with the remaining oil.

5 Bake in a preheated oven for 15-20 minutes, until the fish is cooked through and the butter is melted. Serve with a green salad.

Per serving: 1214kJ/290kcal (15%), 15.1g fat (22%), 5.9g saturates (30%), 1.5g sugars (2%), 0.47g salt (8%)

Cook's tip
Make breadcrumbs whenever you have day-old bread; there's no need to throw it away. Whizz up the bread, including the crust, as it adds flavour and colour, in the food processor and freeze, then you'll have a supply whenever you need it. Frozen, they'll keep for 6 months.

Zarzuela

This sumptuous Catalan fish stew makes a splendid one-course dish for lunch or dinner with friends or family

450g mussels, well scrubbed, from Sainsbury's fish counter 6 tbsp olive oil
3 x 100g monkfish tails, halved, from Sainsbury's fish counter
1 large onion, finely chopped
900g ripe tomatoes, chopped or halved
2 x 390g cartons of chopped tomatoes by Sainsbury's

3 garlic cloves, crushed
3-4 tbsp brandy
4 tbsp ground almonds
1 tsp dried thyme
1 tsp saffron threads (or a generous pinch of ground saffron)
1 tsp smoked paprika
200ml hot fish stock (made with ½ stock cube and boiling water)

4 tbsp dry white wine
juice of ½ lemon
6 frozen raw peeled jumbo king prawns by Sainsbury's
200g frozen squid rings by Sainsbury's, defrosted
12 small scallops by Sainsbury's
2 tbsp chopped flat-leaf parsley
crusty bread, to serve

1 Before you start cooking, prepare the mussels. Scrub the mussels well in cold water, removing beards and any barnacles. Discard any with broken shells or any that do not close tight when tapped on a hard surface.

2 Heat 3 tablespoons of oil in a frying pan over a medium heat. Add the monkfish, cook for 3 minutes, turn over and cook for 3 more minutes. Lift out, cover and set aside.

3 Heat the rest of the oil in the pan, add the onion and fry for 5 minutes, until soft. Add the tomatoes, garlic and brandy, and cook for 5 minutes.

4 Stir in the almonds, thyme, saffron and paprika. Simmer for 5-8 minutes, until most of the liquid has evaporated. Return the monkfish to the pan and coat well with the mixture until piping hot. Season to taste, cover and take off the heat.

5 Bring the stock, wine, 4 tablespoons of water and the lemon juice to the boil in a pan. Add the mussels, reduce the heat, cover and cook for 5 minutes, stirring, until the mussels open. Lift out the mussels and transfer to a colander.

6 Add the prawns to the pan of stock, simmer, add the squid and scallops, and simmer for a further 3-5 minutes, until cooked through. Meanwhile, open the mussels, discarding the shells and any unopened mussels, and then return them to the pan of prawns, squid, scallops and stock.

7 Transfer the contents of the monkfish pan to the pot and stir. Cook for 3-5 minutes or until piping hot. Adjust the seasoning, to taste, scatter over the chopped parsley and serve.

Per serving: 1333kJ/319kcal (16%), 16.6g fat (24%), 2.6g saturates (13%), 10.7g sugars (12%), 1.30g salt (22%)

SERVES 4
PREP 15 minutes
COOK 25–30 minutes,
plus cooling

Baked fish with fennel and lemon

The fish in this fragrant dish is cooked simply, baked in foil with fennel and lemon and drizzled with olive oil and lemon juice

whole white-fleshed fish, such as sea bass or sea bream (about 1.5kg), cleaned but with head, from Sainsbury's fish counter
8 tbsp extra virgin olive oil, plus extra for greasing
$^{1}/_{2}$ lemon, scrubbed and cut into chunks
a handful of fresh fennel fronds or dill
1 tbsp finely chopped fennel fronds or dill (optional)
4 tbsp lemon juice

1 Wipe the fish inside and out with some kitchen paper, removing the dark vein that runs along the back of the cavity. Season to taste inside and out.

2 Preheat the oven to 180°C/160°C fan/gas 4 and set a roasting tin to heat. Lightly oil a sheet of foil, place the fish on it and drizzle 1–2 tablespoons of the oil over it. Tuck the lemon and fennel fronds into the cavity and fold the foil over the fish lengthways, doubling over the top seam to trap the steam. Tuck the ends underneath.

3 Place the fish in the hot tin and bake for 25–30 minutes, depending on the thickness of the fish, until the flesh feels firm when you press it through the foil and is cooked through.

4 Remove from the oven, but do not open the foil. Leave to cool to room temperature. Meanwhile, whisk the oil and lemon juice together with chopped fennel fronds (or dill, if using) and season to taste. Serve this dressing alongside the fish.

Per serving: 1661kJ/399kcal (20%), 27.6g fat (39%), 5.0g saturates (25%), <0.5g sugars (<1%), 0.31g salt (5%)

Why not try?
Experiment with other aromatic herbs, such as oregano, thyme, parsley and basil, instead of the fennel and/or dill.

Barbecued tuna steaks with cucumber and red onion relish

Tuna is a fabulous fish to cook; its robust, meaty texture means that the steaks will hold together well

15cm piece of cucumber

2 tbsp rice wine or white wine vinegar

1 tsp caster sugar

a pinch of dried chilli flakes

¼ red onion, finely sliced

2 x 200g packs of fresh tuna steaks by Sainsbury's

1 tbsp olive oil

1 tsp smoked paprika

lemon or lime wedges, to serve

1 Preheat the grill on its highest setting and prepare a barbecue for cooking. Slice the cucumber in half lengthways and scoop out the seeds with a spoon and discard. Slice each half again lengthways to make 4 long, thin pieces. Then, slice these thinly on the diagonal.

2 In a bowl, whisk together the vinegar, sugar and chilli flakes. Mix through the sliced cucumber and red onion, cover and leave in the fridge to rest for 30 minutes (this softens the taste of the raw onion).

3 Rub each tuna steak on both sides with a little oil and smoked paprika. Cook the tuna under the grill for 2-3 minutes each side and then transfer to the hot barbecue immediately to finish off cooking. Depending on the thickness of the steak, cook for 1-2 minutes each side for medium; 2-3 minutes for well done. The tuna turns opaque as it cooks, and will continue to cook. The fish should be cooked through before serving.

4 Serve the fish with the cucumber relish and a lemon or lime wedge to squeeze over.

Per serving: 750kJ/178kcal (9%), 3.8g fat (5%), 0.7g saturates (4%), 3.1g sugars (3%), 0.63g salt (11%)

Cook's tip

Preparing this cucumber relish a few hours ahead of time will not only save time when finishing the dish but will also help the flavours to blend more.

SERVES 4
PREP 5 minutes,
plus marinating
COOK 6-15 minutes

Spice-rubbed salmon

This simple Cajun-inspired blend of spices livens up any type of fish instantly

1 tsp smoked paprika by Sainsbury's
1 tsp cayenne pepper
½ tsp dried thyme
1 tsp soft light brown sugar

2 x 240g pack of responsibly sourced Scottish salmon fillets by Sainsbury's, skinned
2 tbsp olive oil

1 Combine all of the spices, thyme and sugar in a pestle and mortar or a spice grinder. Grind until you get a fine powder.

2 Rub the mixture over both sides of the fish, cover with cling film and leave to marinate in the fridge for 1 hour, so the flavours can meld with the fish.

3 Preheat the oven to 220°C/200°C fan/gas 7 or preheat the grill on its highest setting. Line a baking tray with baking parchment or line a grill pan with foil.

4 Brush the fish with a little oil on both sides, being careful not to dislodge the spice rub. Bake in a preheated oven for 10-15 minutes or under the grill for 3-4 minutes on each side, depending on thickness, until cooked through and the fish flakes easily.

Per serving: 1214kJ/291kcal (15%), 18.4g fat (26%), 4.4g saturates (22%), 1.9g sugars (2%), 0.84g salt (14%), omega-3 4.7g

Cook's tip
The salmon can be marinated in the rub and frozen, uncooked for 3 months. If you do that, defrost thoroughly before cooking from the start of step 3.

Spices

< Star anise is an eight-pointed star with a strong aniseed flavour and a liquorice-like aroma. Use with leeks, squashes, root vegetables and pulses. It's a spice central to Chinese cooking and a component of Chinese five-spice.

^ Saffron the yellow stigmas of the Sativus crocus are the most expensive spice in the world. Rich pungent, musky and floral. Infuse in water or stock. Use with rice, pasta and most vegetables.

^ Cardamom Use the whole pods, lightly cracked, to impart aroma to rice and curries. Use the seeds inside with pulses, sweet potatoes and root vegetables. Cardamom's floral citrus flavours are great for cutting through fattiness.

< Ginger is available in a variety of forms from fresh, dried, ground and crystallised. It adds a warm, spicy flavour and aroma to bakes. Fresh ginger is essential for curries and most spicy dishes. Ground ginger is hotter than fresh.

> Coriander seeds and ground coriander have a sweet, spicy taste with a hint of aniseed. Once ground the delicate peppery flavour starts to fade, so try grinding seeds when required. Particularly good with mushrooms and onions.

^ Ground cinnamon and cinnamon sticks have a warm sweet scent and flavour. It's used in both sweet and savoury dishes. Use with almonds, tomatoes, rice and other grains.

^ Chilli comes in a variety of different forms from dried and ground, to chopped and as paste and fresh. Ground chilli comes in hot, medium and mild made by grinding dried chillies to a powder.

< Ground turmeric has a rich woody aroma, slightly bitter flavour and intense yellow colour. Essential in Indian curry powders and pastes. Use with pulses, rice, pasta, eggs, beans, aubergines, spinach and potatoes.

^ **Paprika** is ground from dried red sweet peppers, giving a caramel fruitiness. It adds fragrance and colour to tomato - and pulse-based dishes. Smoked paprika has a rich smokiness.

^ **Kaffir lime leaves** have a powerful fragrance between lemon and lime. Use with mushrooms, green vegetables and coconut milk in Thai-style curries

^ **Curry leaves** are also available dried, but fresh leaves offer better flavour. Use with vegetables, lentils and rice. These dark green leaves from a tree of the citrus family, release a nutty, lemony aroma when fried in hot oil.

^ **Cumin seeds** and ground cumin have a strong heavy scent and a rich, slightly earthy flavour. Use with aubergines, beans, root vegetables, potatoes and squashes.

^ **Galangal** has a lemony sourness and a gingery flavour. Use in sauces, curries, soups and stews. Good with chilli, fennel, garlic, shallots and lime. Fresh galangal can be kept wrapped in cling film for 2-3 weeks in the fridge.

^ **Nutmeg** and mace come from the same tree, native to Indonesian islands; nutmeg is the nut and the mace is the outer casing. Add freshly grated nutmeg to add savoury notes to bechamel sauce and aubergine dishes.

< **Tamarind** from the pods of the tamarind tree often used to make a paste. It's an essential ingredient in Worcestershire sauce and adds a fruity tartness to curries and dishes.

< **Garam masala** is a popular pungent spice mix that is likely to include ground coriander, dill seed, cumin, tumeric, cinnamon, black pepper, cloves, ginger and cardamom.

< **Lemongrass** a refreshingly tart spice with a strong citrus flavour. Crush or finely chop for use with most vegetables. Essential in many noodle dishes and Asian curries.

^ **Chinese 5 spice** is a combination of sweet, sour, bitter, pungent and salty spices. The spice mixture is commonly cinnamon, peppercorns, star anise, cloves and fennel seeds.

Short cut to flavour

Single popular spices or those that are more tricky to handle, such as lemongrass, galangal and tamarind, are also available as pastes, as are pastes for more complete dishes such as Thai green curry sauce. Ready-made spice mixes, such as fajita and jerk spices, are becoming increasingly available to get the blends of spice right each time. For more information see sainsburys.co.uk

SERVES 4
PREP 15 minutes
COOK 25 minutes

Fideuà

Think of this Spanish dish as a pasta version of paella. The tasty mixture of fish and seafood makes a delicious dinner

300g mussels from Sainsbury's fish counter

a pinch of saffron threads

750ml hot fish stock (made from 1 stock cube and boiling water)

2-3 tbsp olive oil

1 onion, finely chopped

2 garlic cloves, crushed

3 ripe tomatoes, skinned, deseeded and chopped

1 tsp sweet or smoked paprika

300g spaghetti or linguine, broken into 5cm lengths

225g frozen raw peeled jumbo prawns by Sainsbury's, defrosted

8 small scallops, cut in half

225g firm white fish, such as cod or hake, from Sainsbury's fish counter, cut into 2cm pieces

140g frozen peas

2 tbsp chopped flat-leaf parsley

1 Before you start cooking, prepare the mussels. Scrub the mussels well in cold water, removing beards and any barnacles. Discard any with broken shells or any that do not close tight when tapped on a hard surface.

2 Put the saffron in a small bowl, add 2 tablespoons of the hot stock, cover and set aside.

3 Heat the oil in a large frying or paella pan over a medium heat. Add the onion and garlic and fry for 5-8 minutes, or until soft, stirring frequently. Add the tomatoes and paprika and cook for a further 5 minutes. Add the saffron with its liquid and half the remaining stock, increase the heat and bring to the boil.

4 Add the pasta, reduce to a simmer, uncovered, stirring occasionally, for 5 minutes.

5 Add the prawns, scallops, mussels, white fish and peas. Cook for a further 5 minutes, or until the pasta is cooked and the fish is cooked through; discard any mussels that do not open. If the mixture begins to dry out, add a little more stock. Season to taste, sprinkle with parsley and serve hot, straight from the pan with aïoli (see page 162) and crusty bread.

Per serving: 2299kJ/545kcal (27%), 13.0g fat (19%), 2.5g saturates (13%), 8.1g sugars (9%), 2.37g salt (40%)

Get ahead
The base of the fideuà can be made in advance up to the end of step 2. Pour into a bowl, cool, cover and refrigerate for up to 2 days. Reheat gently, then return to the boil before continuing.

SERVES 4
PREP 10 minutes
COOK 35 minutes,
plus cooling

Grilled white fish with romesco sauce

This Catalan sauce – known as romesco – is perfect to serve with any grilled white fish or seafood. Freeze the leftover sauce for a super-quick spicy partner for any barbecued dishes

4 white fish fillets, such as seabass, from Sainsbury's fish counter

FOR THE SAUCE (SERVES 8)
4 tbsp olive oil
2 red peppers, deseeded and halved

1 red chilli (optional)
350g tomatoes
50g almonds
1 garlic clove
1 tbsp sherry vinegar by Sainsbury's
a handful of fresh parsley, chopped

TO SERVE
500g baby potatoes, larger ones halved
2 x 170g bags of Italian-style salad by Sainsbury's

1 First, make the sauce. Preheat the grill to a medium hot setting. Rub 1 teaspoon of the oil over the peppers and chilli, if using, and place skin-side-up in a grill pan. Rub another teaspoon of oil on the tomatoes and place in the same grill pan.

2 Cook under the grill for 10 minutes. Turn over the tomatoes and add the almonds to the pan. Cook for a further 5 minutes then add the garlic. Grill for a few more minutes until the almonds are lightly toasted, the tomatoes soft and the pepper is blackened.

3 Set aside the almonds and tomatoes. Transfer the peppers to a freezer bag and seal (or put in a bowl and cover). Once cool enough, peel away the blackened skin and discard.

4 Place the pepper flesh in a food processor with the tomatoes and almonds, the sherry vinegar and 3 tablespoons of the oil and whizz until nearly smooth. Stir through the chopped parsley, cover and then set aside until you're ready to serve.

5 Rub the remaining oil over the seabass fillets and season to taste. Heat a barbecue or griddle pan until smoking hot. Place the fillets into the pan skin-side-down and cook for 7 minutes, until the skin is crisp. Carefully turn over and cook for 5 minutes more, or until the fish is cooked through. Serve with the sauce drizzled over and some new potatoes and salad, if you like. (If you freeze the leftover sauce, defrost and use it within 3 months.)

Per serving: 1967kJ/471kcal (24%), 25.9g fat (37%), 3.9g saturates (20%), 10.2g sugars (11%), 0.40g salt (7%)

Did you know?
Sherry vinegar is made in Spain from sherry wine grapes and aged in oak barrels. It is dark brown with a rich and sweetish, nutty flavour. An alternative is red wine vinegar.

Smoked haddock and spinach crumble

This deliciously different fish pie has a savoury crunch with its leek crumble topping

FOR THE CRUMBLE
30g unsalted butter
2 leeks, roughly chopped
175g fresh white bread, roughly torn
3 tbsp chopped parsley leaves
60g Parmesan cheese, grated
60g Scottish porridge oats by Sainsbury's
freshly ground black pepper

FOR THE FILLING
50g unsalted butter
50g plain flour
450ml semi-skimmed milk
juice of ½ lemon
½ tsp ground nutmeg
70g mature Cheddar cheese, grated
100g bag of young leaf spinach by Sainsbury's, roughly chopped

2 x 325g packs of smoked haddock fillets by Sainsbury's, skinned and chopped into bite-sized pieces

1 Preheat the oven to 180°C/160°C fan/gas 4. For the crumble, melt the butter in a large, non-stick frying pan and fry the leeks on a medium-low heat for 10 minutes.

2 Place the bread, parsley and Parmesan in a food processor and process to even-sized crumbs. Add the leeks and pulse until combined, but retaining some texture. Stir in the oats and plenty of pepper.

3 For the filling, melt the butter in a wide, deep, 2-litre flame- and ovenproof dish. Stir in the flour and cook for 2-3 minutes over a medium heat, stirring with a wooden spoon. Then gradually add the milk, stirring.

4 Stir in the lemon juice, nutmeg and Cheddar. Season to taste and stir until the cheese melts. Stir in the spinach, a handful at a time, until wilted. Carefully fold in the fish.

5 Sprinkle the crumble over the top and place on a baking tray. Bake in a preheated oven, uncovered, for 20 minutes.

Per serving: 1936kJ/463kcal (23%), 21.9g fat (31%), 12.4g saturates (62%), 6.5g sugars (7%), 1.83g salt (31%)

Grilled fish with butter beans and chorizo

Delicate white fish works really well with the contrasting flavours of chorizo sausage and the butter beans

1 tbsp olive oil

100g chorizo, chopped

1 garlic clove, crushed

2 x 400g tins butter beans by Sainsbury's, drained and rinsed

finely grated zest and juice of ½ lemon

1 roasted red pepper, chopped

3 tablespoons lighter crème fraîche by Sainsbury's

4 boneless white fish fillets (about 150g each), from Sainsbury's fish counter

a handful of fresh parsley, chopped

1 Heat most of the oil in medium-sized pan (leave a little oil to rub on the fish). Add the chorizo and cook for 2–3 minutes, until the chorizo is lightly crisp and the oil has started to run. Add the garlic and cook for 30 seconds followed by the butter beans, 200ml water and the lemon zest. Bring to the boil, then reduce the heat to a simmer.

2 Add the red pepper and crème fraîche and leave to bubble until the beans are heated through and the liquid has mostly boiled away. Then, squeeze over a little of the lemon juice and season to taste. Cover and set aside.

3 Preheat the grill to hot. Rub the remaining oil over the fish and season to taste.

4 Place the fish skin-side-up in a grill pan and cook under the hot grill for 5–7 minutes, until the skin is golden. Carefully turn over and cook for a further 5 minutes, until the fish is cooked through and flakes away easily.

5 Reheat the sauce, stir through some parsley and serve alongside the fish. This dish is great served with some crusty bread and a green salad.

Per serving: 1688kJ/401kcal (20%), 13.2g fat (19%), 4.6g saturates (23%), 4.9g sugars (5%), 1.17g salt (20%)

SERVES 4
PREP 10 minutes,
plus chilling
COOK 55 minutes

Crispy polenta fish fingers with easy tartare sauce

The light polenta coating on these home-made fish fingers gives them a lovely crunchy finish

400g skinless, firm-fleshed
white fish steak, such as coley
or cod (available in the
frozen section)
2 tbsp plain flour
1 egg, lightly beaten
100g fine polenta by Sainsbury's
sunflower oil, for frying

FOR THE TARTARE SAUCE
2 gherkins, coarsely grated
6 heaped tbsp mayonnaise
by Sainsbury's
1 tbsp white wine vinegar
1 tbsp capers, very finely chopped
finely grated zest of $1/2$ lemon
1 heaped tbsp finely chopped dill

FOR THE POTATO WEDGES
750g Maris Piper potatoes,
peeled and cut into wedges
1 tbsp olive oil

1 Cut the fish into 2cm thick strips. Pat it dry with kitchen paper. Lay out the flour, egg and polenta in three shallow bowls.

2 Coat the fish fingers by dusting them first with the flour, then dipping them in the egg, then rolling them in the polenta, until they are well covered. Put them on a plate, cover with cling film and chill for 30 minutes (this helps the coating to stick).

3 Preheat the oven to 200°C/180°C fan/gas 6. Meanwhile, place the potato wedges on a baking tray and drizzle over the oil and toss the potatoes to coat, then season to taste. Bake for 45–50 minutes, until cooked through and golden, turning halfway.

4 Next, make the tartare sauce. First, put the grated gherkins on to a chopping board and chop again, finely, with a sharp knife. Mix the gherkins, mayonnaise, wine vinegar, capers, lemon zest and dill. Cover and chill until needed.

5 Heat a large, deep-sided frying pan and add enough oil to cover the base. To test the oil is hot enough, place a small cube of bread into the oil and if it colours straightaway then the correct temperature has been reached. Fry the fish fingers for 2 minutes on each side, turning carefully, until golden and crisp all over. Rest them on a plate lined with kitchen paper while you cook the remainder. These fish fingers go perfectly with the home-made chunky potato wedges and the tartare sauce.

Per serving: 3038kJ/730kcal (37%), 50.9g fat (73%), 5.5g saturates (28%), 2.1g sugars (2%), 1.23g salt (21%)

Cook's tip
Using polenta is an alternative to breadcrumbs when it comes to frying fish. The dry texture of polenta gives you a far crisper finish. Add a seasoning, such as 1 tsp smoked paprika, to the polenta, if you like.

Tarte au poissons

All kinds of cooked fish work well for this tart – trout, salmon,
cod and haddock as well as smoked fish and cooked prawns

375g ready-rolled light
shortcrust pastry by Sainsbury's
plain flour, for dusting
1 onion, finely chopped
45g Butterlicious spread
by Sainsbury's
4 ripe tomatoes, skinned,
deseeded and diced
1 small garlic clove, crushed
2 tsp chopped thyme leaves

a large pinch of freshly
grated nutmeg
150ml lighter créme fraîche
by Sainsbury's
2 eggs, beaten
175g cooked fish, pin-boned,
skinned and flaked into
large pieces
1 tbsp grated Gruyère cheese

1 Preheat the oven to 180°C/160°C fan/gas 4. Line a 20cm flan ring or tart tin with
greaseproof paper or baking parchment.

2 Lay the pastry out on a floured surface, and roll out if need be, so that you have
a 25cm pastry circle to lay into the prepared flan ring or tart tin. Chill for 15 minutes.

3 Line the tart tin with the pastry. Line the pastry case with greaseproof & non-stick baking
paper by Sainsbury's and fill with baking beans. Bake for 12–15 minutes, or until cooked. Lift
out the paper and beans and return to the oven for a further 5 minutes to crisp. Then,
remove the pastry case from the oven and allow to cool. Meanwhile, reduce
the oven temperature to 150°C/130°C fan/gas 2.

4 Cook the onion in the spread for 4–5 minutes, or until translucent. Add the tomatoes
and garlic, then cool. Stir in the thyme, nutmeg, cream and eggs.

5 Arrange the fish in the pastry case and spoon over the mixture and sprinkle over
the Gruyère. Return the tart to the oven and bake for 25–35 minutes, or until it's set
and golden. Serve warm or cold.

Per serving: 2714kJ/650kcal (33%), 38.5g fat (55%), 18.6g saturates (93%),
6.1g sugars (7%), 1.15g salt (19%)

Cook's tip
Use up any leftover pastry to make mini strawberry
jam tarts or lemon curd tarts to have for pudding.

Prawn gumbo

A classic treat from Louisiana, this prawn stew has a brown roux base and is thickened with okra, also known as gumbo

85g Butterlicious spread
by Sainsbury's
3 x 350g packs of large peeled
prawns by Sainsbury's
100g white and brown crabmeat
Taste the Difference
2 tbsp plain flour
1/2 tsp cayenne pepper
1 large onion, finely chopped
2 garlic cloves, grated or
finely chopped
115g okra, trimmed

1 large red pepper, deseeded
and diced
2 x 390g cartons of tomatoes
by Sainsbury's or 750g fresh
tomatoes, halved
1 litre hot fish or shellfish stock
(made with 1/2 fish stock cube
and boiling water)
1 bay leaf
2 sprigs of fresh thyme
finely grated zest of 1 lemon

TO SERVE
500g basmati rice
hot pepper sauce

1 Melt the butter in a large saucepan, add the prawns in batches and stir-fry over
a medium heat for 2-3 minutes, or until cooked through. Lift on to a plate and cool.

2 Add the crab and flour to the butter, cook over a low heat for 3-4 minutes, or until the
flour is golden. Add the cayenne pepper, onion and garlic, and cook for a further 3 minutes.

3 Stir in the okra and red pepper. Pour over the tomatoes, stock, herbs and lemon zest.
Bring to the boil and simmer for 25-30 minutes until thick.

4 Stir the prawns into the gumbo to heat through and season to taste. Serve with basmati
rice, cooked to the pack instructions, and a splash of hot pepper sauce.

Per serving: 1783kJ/422kcal (21%), 8.6g fat (12%), 3.0g saturates (15%), 5.9g sugars
(7%), 2.61g salt (44%)

Salmon jungle curry

The hot, fresh flavours of this quick-to-make fish curry also work well with monkfish and with leftover chicken or turkey

2 tbsp vegetable oil

2 tbsp Thai green curry paste by Sainsbury's

3 garlic cloves, crushed

5cm fresh root ginger, peeled and grated

2 hot red chillies, deseeded and shredded

400g tin coconut milk light by Sainsbury's

225g drained bamboo shoots, drained and rinsed

a good splash of fish sauce

2 heaped tbsp pea aubergines (available in jars)

75g baby corn, halved lengthways

2 x 240g pack of responsibly sourced Scottish salmon fillets by Sainsbury's, skinned and cut into chunks

a small handful of fresh basil leaves (preferably Thai basil)

240g Thai jasmine rice by Sainsbury's, to serve

1 In a large frying pan, heat the oil, add the curry paste and stir. Add the garlic, ginger and chillies. Keep stirring for 2-3 minutes.

2 Pour in the coconut milk. Bring to the boil then add the bamboo shoots, fish sauce, pea aubergines and baby corn. Reduce the heat slightly and simmer for 5 minutes.

3 Add the salmon followed by the basil leaves. Continue to simmer for a further 10 minutes, or until the fish is cooked through, then season to taste. Serve with Thai jasmine rice, cooked according to the pack instructions.

Per serving: 2188kJ/509kcal (26%), 27.2g fat (39%), 9.7g saturates (49%), 4.6g sugars (5%), 3.10g salt (52%)

Get ahead

Make this curry sauce the day before. Just cover it and keep in the fridge. Return to a simmer before adding the fish.

SERVES 4
PREP 10 minutes
COOK 4-6 minutes

Grilled herring with mustard butter

Herring brunch recipes often use bacon and oatmeal, but the mustard here makes this a great dish for any meal. This recipe also works with sprats, mackerel, sardines or trout

8 herrings, from Sainsbury's fish counter, scaled, gutted and trimmed, with heads removed
1 tbsp vegetable oil
115g bunch of watercress (or 2 x 50g bags of pea shoots), to garnish
lemon halves, to garnish

FOR THE MUSTARD BUTTER
75g unsalted butter, softened, plus extra for grilling
1 tbsp wholegrain mustard
1 tsp thyme leaves
a splash of lemon juice

1 Preheat the grill on its highest setting. Wash and pat the herrings dry with kitchen paper, brush with oil and season to taste. Place on a sheet of lightly buttered foil in a grill pan.

2 To make the mustard butter, simply mix the butter, mustard and thyme together. Add a little lemon juice and season to taste.

3 Grill the herrings for 2-3 minutes on each side or until cooked through; they will be firm to the touch. Then, lift the herrings on to a large, warmed serving dish and dot the mustard butter over the fish. Garnish with watercress (or pea shoots) and lemon wedges.

Per serving: 2320kJ/559kcal (28%), 45.1g fat (64%), 16.1g saturates (81%), <0.5g sugars (<1%), 0.79g salt (13%)

Get ahead
To save some time on the day, the mustard butter can be made, wrapped in baking parchment and chilled 1-2 days in advance.

SERVES 4
PREP 10 minutes
COOK 35 minutes

Salmon, horseradish and kale bake

Kale is readily available these days and makes a wonderful dish partnered with horseradish and salmon as here

2 x 240g pack of responsibly sourced Scottish salmon fillets by Sainsbury's, skinned
600ml semi-skimmed milk
2 handfuls of kale, stalks trimmed and leaves roughly chopped

30g unsalted butter
1 tbsp plain flour
115g mature Cheddar cheese, grated
1-2 tbsp creamed horseradish sauce by Sainsbury's

1 Preheat the oven to 200°C/180°C fan/gas 6.

2 Place the salmon fillets in a frying pan and pour in enough milk to cover them. Poach gently over a low heat for about 10 minutes, until opaque and cooked through, then transfer the fillets to an ovenproof dish using a slotted spoon or fish slice. Strain and reserve the milk.

3 Boil or steam the kale for about 5 minutes, until nearly soft, then drain and add to the ovenproof dish with the salmon.

4 Melt the butter in a saucepan and stir in the flour. Cook for 1 minute, until foaming, then gradually add the poaching milk, whisking constantly to avoid any lumps forming.

5 Bring to the boil, stirring, for 4-5 minutes, until thickened. Remove from the heat and add the cheese, stirring, until it melts, then stir in the horseradish sauce.

6 Pour this piquant sauce over the salmon and kale, and bake in a preheated oven for about 15 minutes, until golden.

Per serving: 2135kJ/512kcal (26%), 32.5g fat (46%), 15.0g saturates (75%), 10.3g sugars (11%), 1.93g salt (32%)

Get ahead
The whole dish can be assembled, covered and chilled several hours in advance. Simply bring to room temperature before baking.

SERVES 4
PREP 10 minutes
COOK 30 minutes

Prawns stewed with chilli tomato sauce and feta

This Greek-inspired dish is an unusual pairing of tasty prawns and tangy feta cheese, but one that works well

1 tbsp olive oil

1 onion, finely chopped

2 garlic cloves, chopped

125ml dry white wine

390g carton of chopped tomatoes by Sainsbury's

a handful of fresh oregano leaves, chopped (or a pinch of dried oregano)

a pinch of dried chilli flakes

400g frozen raw peeled jumbo king prawns by Sainsbury's, defrosted

75g feta cheese

a handful of fresh parsley, chopped

240g basmati rice, cooked according to pack instructions, to serve

1 Heat the olive oil in a casserole dish or heavy-based saucepan over a medium heat. Add the onion and cook for 5 minutes, or until softened, then stir in the chopped garlic and cook for a further minute.

2 Pour over the wine and let it bubble away for a few minutes. Then, add the tomatoes followed by the oregano, chilli flakes and 200ml of water.

3 Bring to the boil and then reduce to a simmer and cook for 10 minutes. Add the prawns to the pan and cook for a further 5 minutes, until cooked through. Finally, sprinkle over the feta cheese and parsley before serving with the cooked basmati rice.

Per serving: 1785kJ/423kcal (21%), 10.4g fat (15%), 4.1g saturates (21%), 6.0g sugars (7%), 1.9g salt (32%)

Why not try?

Make a spicy prawn, feta and tomato salad using similar flavours. Whisk together 1 tbsp red wine vinegar, 3 tbsp extra virgin olive oil and ½ chilli, deseeded and finely chopped, until smooth. Toss together some cooked prawns, cherry tomatoes, small cubes of feta and shredded Romaine lettuce leaves in a large bowl in the dressing, adding a scattering of oregano before serving.

Sole Colbert

This French Escoffier classic is traditionally served with pont neuf (very thin chips); this recipe also works with any small flat fish, such as plaice or lemon sole

a little vegetable oil
for shallow-frying
2 tbsp plain flour
4 small boneless Dover sole
fillets, from Sainsbury's fish
counter, skinned
1 egg, beaten
6 tbsp dried white breadcrumbs

170g bag of Italian-style salad
by Sainsbury's

FOR PONT NEUF
375g Maris Piper potatoes,
peeled and cut into
narrow batons
1 tbsp vegetable oil

**FOR THE MAÎTRE
D'HÔTEL BUTTER**
60g unsalted butter, softened
3 tbsp finely chopped
flat-leaf parsley
lemon juice, to taste

1 Preheat the oven to 200°C/180°C fan/gas 6. Meanwhile, place the potato batons on a baking tray, drizzle over the oil and toss the potatoes to coat; season to taste.

2 Bake for 35-40 minutes, turning halfway, and checking regularly. Cook until golden.

3 Meanwhile, mix all the ingredients for the maître d'hôtel butter, adding lemon juice and seasoning to taste. Roll into a sausage shape, wrap in cling film and chill.

4 Heat the oil in a large pan.

5 Season the flour to taste and dust the fish evenly in it. Brush thoroughly with the egg and then roll the fish in the breadcrumbs.

6 Fry the sole for 3-4 minutes on each side; it will curl slightly and be golden and cooked through. Lift on to kitchen paper briefly before arranging on a serving dish.

7 Cut the butter into 0.5cm slices and put 1-2 slices on each fish. It will melt to create a lovely, slightly rich, dressing. Serve with pont neuf and salad.

Per serving: 3340kJ/809kcal (41%), 38.0g fat (54%), 16.0g saturates (80%), 3.3g sugars (4%), 1.08g salt (18%)

Get ahead
Make the maître d'hôtel butter 2–3 days beforehand and keep chilled until ready to use.

Prawn, pepper and tomato kebabs

One of the most popular ways to enjoy jumbo prawns caught off the coast in the Eastern Mediterranean region is to grill them on skewers with a mixture of colourful vegetables

juice of 2 lemons, plus
1 additional lemon, cut into
wedges, to serve
4 garlic cloves, crushed
1 tsp ground cumin
1 tsp smoked paprika

16 frozen raw peeled jumbo king
prawns by Sainsbury's, defrosted
8-12 cherry tomatoes
1 green pepper, deseeded and
cut into bite-sized squares
vegetable oil, for greasing

1 Mix together the lemon juice, garlic, cumin and paprika and rub the mixture over the prawns. Cover and leave the prawns to marinate for 30 minutes.

2 Meanwhile, prepare the barbecue or preheat the grill to its hottest setting. Thread the prawns onto metal skewers, alternating with the tomatoes and green pepper pieces, until all the ingredients are used.

3 Cook the kebabs on an oiled rack over a barbecue (or under the grill) for 2-3 minutes on each side, basting with the rest of the marinade, until the prawns are tender and cooked through and the tomatoes and peppers are lightly coloured. Be careful when turning as the skewers will be hot. Serve immediately with lemon wedges.

Per serving: 324kJ/77kcal (4%), 2.4g fat (3%), 0.4g saturates (2%), 3.2g sugars (4%), 0.19g salt (3%)

Why not try?
Use different ingredients instead of the peppers and tomatoes. Alternate the shellfish with thick pieces of onion, whole cloves of garlic, chunks of celery or lemon wedges, in any combination you like.

Miso-marinated salmon with greens and rice

The flavours of Japan offer a delicious way to cook salmon and one that is packed full of 'umami', a pleasant savoury taste

5 tbsp miso soup paste
by Sainsbury's
3 tbsp mirin (rice wine)
by Sainsbury's
1 tbsp sugar
2 x 240g pack of responsibly
sourced Scottish salmon fillets
by Sainsbury's
a little vegetable oil, for greasing

TO SERVE
240g basmati rice
200g Oriental greens, such
as pak choi

1 Stir together the miso paste, mirin and sugar until smooth. Then transfer to a large freezer bag or a large shallow bowl.

2 Place the salmon in the bag or bowl and mix together with the sauce until completely covered. Then seal the bag or cover the bowl with cling film. Leave in the fridge to marinate for at least 2 hours and up to 24 hours.

3 Preheat the oven to 200°C/180°C fan/gas 6 and line a shallow baking dish with foil (this will make your clear-up so much easier), then lightly grease the foil.

4 Pick up the fish, shaking away any excess marinade, but making sure you leave a thin coating on the fish and transfer to the foil-lined dish. Cook in a preheated oven for 15 minutes, until the top is golden and the fish is cooked through and flakes easily. Serve simply with basmati rice, cooked according to the pack instructions, and steamed pak choi.

Per serving: 2383kJ/566kcal (28%), 18.8g fat (27%), 4.8g saturates (24%), 8.5g sugars (9%), 1.79g salt (30%)

Did you know?
Miso is a traditional Japanese paste made from fermenting soya beans and sometimes rice or barley. There are a wide range of varieties, the most common being the milder-tasting and pale-looking white miso and the darker red or brown miso. Mirin is a sweetened form of the famous Japanese rice wine, sake.

Meat

Poultry

Beef

Pork

Lamb

Bourbon and brown sugar barbecue chicken

A classic barbecue sauce is given a lift with the addition of bourbon, or whisky, for a deep, smoky flavour

250g tomato ketchup
200ml cider vinegar
60ml bourbon whisky or blended whisky by Sainsbury's
100g light soft brown sugar
1 tsp mustard powder

1 tsp cayenne pepper or paprika
1 tsp garlic powder
8 chicken thighs

TO SERVE
350g portion per person of Boston baked beans (see p148)
100g young leaf spinach
400g sweetcorn cobs

1 Preheat the grill to a medium hot setting (or preheat the oven to 180°C/160°C fan/gas 4 if you plan to cook it in the oven).

2 Meanwhile, in a medium bowl, whisk together the ketchup, vinegar, bourbon (or whisky), sugar and spices. Set aside some of the sauce for glazing later and then generously baste the chicken with the rest.

3 Cook the chicken under a medium-hot grill, basting regularly, for 12-15 minutes on each side, or until cooked through, with no pink remaining; or cook the chicken in the oven for 25-30 minutes, again basting often, or until cooked through, with no pink remaining.

4 Using a clean brush, baste the reserved sauce all over the cooked chicken thighs. Serve hot with some sides of Boston baked beans, spinach and sweetcorn cobs.

Per serving: 4341kJ/1035kcal (52%), 40.1g fat (57%), 11.6g saturates (58%), 74.8g sugars (83%), 1.16g salt (19%)

Turkey tetrazzini

This easy-to-make, comforting bake is a perfect dish
to enjoy with friends and family

500g dried pasta, such
as spaghetti, penne or fusilli

3 tbsp unsalted butter

4 garlic cloves, crushed

500g onion, chopped

100g button mushrooms, sliced

250ml white wine

750ml hot chicken stock
(made with 1 stock cube and
boiling water)

50g plain flour

100ml lighter créme fraîche
by Sainsbury's

250ml skimmed milk

400g cooked turkey, shredded

1 tsp ground nutmeg

300g lighter mature Cheddar
cheese by Sainsbury's, grated

100g Parmesan cheese, grated

225g frozen peas

juice of 1 lemon

70g panko breadcrumbs

1 Cook the pasta according to the pack instructions. Drain, cover and set aside.

2 Melt the butter in a large frying pan. Add the garlic and onions and sauté for 5-7 minutes,
until the onions are soft. Stir in the mushrooms and cook for a further 5 minutes, stirring.

3 Stir in the wine and 500ml of the stock, reduce the heat to a simmer and allow the liquid
to reduce for 10 minutes. Then, add the flour, stir to incorporate and pour in the remaining
stock a little at a time, whisking it into a sauce.

4 Preheat the oven to 180°C/160°C fan/gas 4.

5 Reduce the heat to medium-low. Stir in the cream, milk, shredded turkey, nutmeg and
both lots of cheese. Season to taste, mix thoroughly and simmer for 15-20 minutes. Then
stir in the cooked pasta along with the peas.

6 Remove the pan from the heat and stir in the lemon juice. Transfer the mixture from the
pan to a casserole and top with the breadcrumbs. Bake for 25 minutes, or until golden and
bubbling. Serve hot.

Per serving: 2171kJ/516kcal (26%), 17.1g fat (24%), 10.0g saturates (50%), 7.4g sugars
(8%), 1.63g salt (27%)

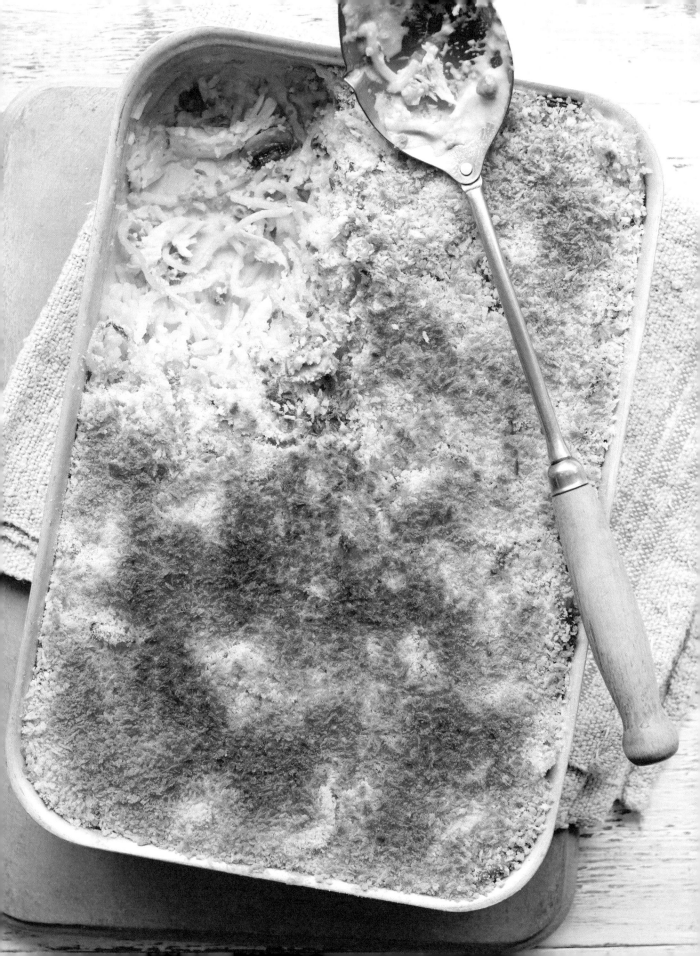

SERVES 6
PREP 20-30 minutes,
plus chilling
COOK 40-50 minutes

Buffalo chicken wings

Hailing from Buffalo, New York, these sweet and spicy chicken wings are easy to prepare and make excellent finger food, served here with a traditional blue cheese dressing

130g plain flour
150g fresh breadcrumbs
1 tsp paprika
½ tsp cayenne pepper
400ml buttermilk by Sainsbury's
24 chicken wings
1-2 tbsp sunflower oil, for frying

FOR THE SAUCE
250ml hot chilli sauce
2 garlic cloves, chopped
2 tbsp runny honey
115g Butterlicious spread by Sainsbury's

FOR THE DRESSING
50g reduced-fat mayonnaise by Sainsbury's

100g Be good to yourself soured cream by Sainsbury's
80ml buttermilk by Sainsbury's
100g blue cheese, such as Stilton, crumbled
30ml cider vinegar by Sainsbury's
chopped flat-leaf parsley, to garnish

1 Place the flour, breadcrumbs, paprika and cayenne pepper in a large bowl and mix to combine. Place the buttermilk in a separate bowl. Dip the chicken wings in the buttermilk. Then toss them in the flour mixture, making sure each one is evenly coated and shaking off any excess. Cover and chill the coated chicken wings in the fridge for at least 1 hour.

2 Preheat the oven to 200°C/180°C fan/gas 6. For the sauce, place the hot chilli sauce, garlic, honey and butter in a pan on a low heat. Let the butter melt, then reduce the heat to a simmer and cook for 5 minutes. Remove from the heat, cover, set aside and keep warm.

3 Place the chicken wings in a shallow roasting tin and roast in the oven for 12-14 minutes, or until the chicken is cooked through, with no pink remaining. Then, heat the oil in a large frying pan and fry the chicken wings for 5 minutes, turning occasionally, until they have a golden colour. You will need to do this in batches to avoid overcrowding the pan.

4 Dip the chicken wings in the warm barbecue sauce. Turn them through the mixture to ensure that they are evenly coated on all sides. Place on a wire rack to cool.

5 For the dressing, place all the ingredients in a food processor and pulse until combined. Serve the dressing in a small bowl alongside the chicken wings.

Per serving: 3624kJ/867kcal (43%), 47.7g fat (68%), 15.1g saturates (76%), 23.6g sugars (26%), 2.64g salt (44%)

Cook's tip
You can make your own buttermilk at home. Combine 1 tbsp lemon juice or vinegar with 250ml semi-skimmed milk. Let it stand for 10 minutes before using.

Oils and vinegars

Groundnut oil >
This useful oil is made from peanuts. It's virtually flavourless, retaining only a slightly nutty taste. It has a high heat resistance, making it good for frying and stir-frying.

Grapeseed oil >
Pressed from the seeds of grapes, this oil has a clean, light taste that makes it great for frying. It also can be cooked at a relatively high temperature, so perfect for giving a crispy coating.

> Sesame oil Made using toasted sesame seeds, it has a distinctive nutty roasted taste. Best used to drizzle over oriental dishes or salads before serving.

Extra virgin olive oil >
The best olive oil has an excellent rich flavour and an intense dark green or dark gold colour. Use for dressings and for dipping bread rather than for cooking as it gets quite smoky when heated.

^ Sunflower oil A good all-purpose oil for cooking and light dressings. This oil has been the UK favourite for decades due to its neutrality and versatility. Suitable for deep-frying.

^ Rapeseed oil Fast becoming a favourite among professional chefs, this oil is a lighter alternative to other cooking oils and is produced in the UK. Use rapeseed oil both when cooking and when making salad dressing.

Walnut oil ^
Rich and flavoursome with a distinctive walnut flavour, walnut oil has many uses: in salad dressings, drizzled over pasta or with vegetables and in stir-fries.

Balsamic vinegar >
This dark-brown syrupy vinegar has a smooth sweet-sour flavour. It's made only in the Modena region of Italy from reduced grape juice that is aged in wooden casks. Use for sauces, gravies and salad dressings.

^ Sherry vinegar
This vinegar is made from the 'must', the freshly pressed unfermented juice, of the sherry grape. It is golden and has a deep complex flavour, which is rich, nutty and sweetish. Use in stews, sauces and casseroles.

< Red wine vinegar
Like white wine vinegar it is made from the natural fermentation process in this case of red wine. The colour ranges, depending on which wine is used. Its tart sharp taste means it's great in dressings, sauces and in pickling.

^ White wine vinegar
Made by the natural fermentation of white wine; its colour ranges, depending on the wine used. Its sharp, tart taste works well in salsas, marinades and sauces.

Olive oil >
This staple ingredient of the Mediterranean diet is now in most British storecupboards. Olive oil is hugely versatile: it can be used in cooking as well in salad dressings. Use as a base for marinades, for grilling, shallow-frying, in sauces and breads.

Dirty rice

A classic recipe from America's Deep South, this dish gets its name from the colour given by the meat

4 tbsp olive oil

1 onion, finely chopped

½ celery stick, finely chopped

1 green pepper, deseeded and finely chopped

200g chicken livers by Sainsbury's, trimmed and finely chopped

250g minced pork

1 green chilli, deseeded and finely chopped

2 garlic cloves, finely chopped

1 tsp smoked paprika by Sainsbury's

1 tsp coriander seeds, crushed

300g long-grain white rice

750ml hot chicken stock (made from 1 chicken stock cube and boiling water)

a large sprig of fresh thyme

a handful of fresh flat-leaf parsley, finely chopped

1 tbsp finely chopped oregano leaves

1 Preheat the oven to 160°C/140°C fan/gas 3.

2 Heat 3 tablespoons of the oil in a large flameproof casserole. Add the onion, celery and pepper. Cook for 5 minutes, until soft. Remove from the casserole, cover and set aside.

3 Pour the remaining oil into the casserole and increase the heat to high. Add the chicken livers and the pork. Cook for about 5 minutes, turning occasionally, until the meat has taken on a good colour. Then, add the chilli, garlic, smoked paprika and crushed coriander seeds. Cook for a further 2 minutes.

4 Return the vegetables to the casserole and stir in the rice. Then add the hot stock and thyme, and bring to the boil. Stir the rice mixture well, cover and transfer to the oven. Cook for 30-40 minutes, stirring occasionally, until the rice is cooked and the stock absorbed.

5 Remove from the oven and leave to rest for about 5 minutes. Remove and discard the thyme. Stir in the chopped herbs, taste and adjust the seasoning, if needed. Serve hot.

Per serving: 1546kJ/380kcal (19%), 13.5g fat (19%), 3.4g saturates (17%), 2.6g sugars (3%), 0.90g salt (15%)

Cook's tip
Freeze the remaining half of the chicken livers pack to make this dish another time; use within 6 months. Don't refreeze them, though, if you bought and used frozen livers initially.

Chicken and coconut curry

Get ahead by marinating the chicken for this delicious Thai curry the night before; the flavours will deepen, too

FOR THE MARINADE
2 lemongrass stalks
3 garlic cloves, finely chopped
1 red chilli, finely chopped
2 tbsp Madras curry paste
by Sainsbury's
1 tbsp dark brown sugar
3 tbsp soy sauce reduced salt
by Sainsbury's

FOR THE CURRY
450g chicken thigh fillets,
cut into strips
½ tbsp vegetable oil
1 red onion, finely chopped
150ml hot chicken stock
(made with ½ stock cube and
boiling water)
400ml tin coconut milk light
by Sainsbury's

1 aubergine, cut into 2cm cubes
2 courgettes, cut into 2cm cubes
fresh basil leaves, to garnish
240g Thai jasmine rice by
Sainsbury's, to serve

1 Peel the lemongrass stalks to reveal the soft white centres; discard the tough outer layers and trim the top and the base of the stalks. Roughly chop the tender white inner layers of the lemongrass and place in a mini food processor with the rest of the marinade ingredients. Blend well to a smooth paste, trying to remove all lumps as far as possible.

2 Place the chicken strips in a shallow dish and spoon over the marinade, stirring to coat thoroughly. Cover and set aside to marinate for 1 hour at room temperature; you may marinate the chicken for up to a day, but do so then in the fridge.

3 Heat a large, non-stick frying pan that has a lid over a high heat, add the oil and reduce the temperature to medium. Add the onion and fry for 5 minutes, stirring occasionally, until softened but not coloured. Add the chicken and its marinade and fry for a further 5 minutes, stirring occasionally to colour the chicken on all sides.

4 Pour in the stock and coconut milk, then add the aubergine and courgettes. Season to taste, bring to the boil, cover then reduce the heat and simmer gently for 15-20 minutes, until the chicken is cooked through, with no pink remaining. Scatter with basil leaves and serve with Thai jasmine rice, cooked according to the pack instructions.

Per serving: 2151kJ/513kcal (26%), 23.2g fat (33%), 9.45g saturates (47%), 14.5g sugars (16%), 3.75g salt (63%)

Duck cassoulet

This indulgent dish, originating in France, is named after the earthenware pot in which it was traditionally cooked

150g unsmoked bacon medallions Be good to yourself, cut into cubes

4 Cumberland sausages Be good to yourself, about 200g in total

6 duck legs

1 tbsp olive oil

2 onions, chopped

4 garlic cloves, crushed

200g carrots, peeled and cut into cubes

1 tbsp chopped thyme

1 tbsp oregano leaves

1 bay leaf

400g tomatoes, diced

250ml white wine

500ml hot chicken stock (made with ¹/₂ stock cube and boiling water)

2 x 410g tins haricot beans, drained and rinsed

50g Butterlicious spread by Sainsbury's

100g fresh breadcrumbs

1 Place the pancetta, sausages and duck legs in a large, flameproof casserole. Cook the meat over a medium heat for 10-15 minutes, until coloured all over. Remove all the meat with a slotted spoon, cover and set aside. Preheat the oven to 150°C/130°C fan/gas 2.

2 Add the oil to the casserole followed by the onions and garlic, and cook for 5 minutes over a medium heat, until the onions are starting to colour. Add the carrots, thyme, oregano and bay leaf and stir well to incorporate. Cook for a further 2-3 minutes.

3 Stir in the tomatoes, wine, stock and beans. Return the meat to the casserole, bring to the boil and then remove from the heat.

4 Place the butter and breadcrumbs in a bowl and mix to combine. Spread the breadcrumb mixture evenly over the casserole. Bake, uncovered, in the oven for 3 hours. Serve hot.

Per serving: 3277kJ/788kcal (39%), 57.7g fat (82%), 16.9g saturates (85%), 9.6g sugars (11%), 2.00g salt (33%)

Why not try?
Mix up some new flavours using this cooking technique. For a pork cassoulet, for instance, use pork loin in place of the duck legs and substitute half the haricot beans with red kidney beans. Cook as above and serve hot.

Spicy stir-fried chicken with vegetables

This dish has a spicy kick, but the amount of chilli can be reduced, if you prefer, for a milder but still tasty version

3 tbsp soy sauce reduced salt by Sainsbury's

2 tbsp rice wine or dry sherry

1 tsp caster sugar

2½ tbsp sunflower oil

460g chicken thigh fillets by Sainsbury's, cut into 1cm strips

50g fine green beans, trimmed and halved

50g broccoli florets

2 garlic cloves, crushed

3cm fresh root ginger, peeled and finely chopped

1 red chilli, deseeded and finely chopped

a bunch of spring onions, cut into 2cm pieces

100g sugarsnap peas, halved on the diagonal

1 tbsp oyster sauce

1 Make the marinade by mixing 1 tablespoon of the soy sauce, 1 tablespoon of the rice wine (or sherry), the sugar and ½ tablespoon of the oil in a bowl.

2 Add the chicken strips to the bowl of marinade, mix around to coat then cover with cling film and refrigerate for 30 minutes to let the flavours mingle.

3 Cook the green beans in a pan of boiling water for 1 minute. Add the broccoli and cook for a further minute. Drain and refresh under cold running water. Cover and set aside.

4 Heat the remaining oil in a wok, add the garlic, ginger and chilli. Fry for 1 minute. Now add the chicken and stir for 2–3 minutes before adding the spring onions and sugarsnaps. Stir-fry for a further 2–3 minutes, or until the chicken is cooked through, with no pink remaining.

5 Pour in the remaining soy sauce and rice wine along with the oyster sauce, and bring to the boil. Finally, add the vegetables and heat through to serve.

Per serving: 1384kJ/332kcal (17%), 14.3g fat (28%), 4.3g saturates (22%), 6.2g sugars (7%), 1.61g salt (27%)

Why not try?
Leave out the chicken or replace it with tofu for a meat-free stir-fry. Cut the same quantity of tofu into cubes and marinate for as long as you can before cooking as above.

Chicken Adobo

This celebrated Filipino dish brings together the flavours of soy sauce, the tang of vinegar and the fragrance of bay leaf

1 tbsp olive oil
3 x 460g packs chicken thighs
by Sainsbury's
500g white onions, sliced
into rings
4 garlic cloves, crushed
1 tbsp arrowroot

1 tbsp freshly ground
black pepper
125ml white wine vinegar
125ml soy sauce reduced salt
by Sainsbury's
juice of 3 limes
1 bay leaf

1 Heat the oil in a large, heavy-based pan. Add the chicken and cook for 5-6 minutes on each side, until coloured all over. Do this in batches to avoid overcrowding the pan. Remove with a slotted spoon, cover and set aside.

2 Add the onions, garlic, arrowroot and pepper to the pan. Toss to coat the onions, then return the chicken to the pan. Pour in the vinegar, soy sauce, lime juice and add the bay leaf.

3 Reduce the heat to a simmer and cook uncovered for 45 minutes, or until the chicken has cooked through, with no pink remaining. Remove the bay leaf. This dish is delicious simply spooned hot over plain basmati rice.

Per serving: 1928kJ/463kcal (23%), 31.1g fat (44%), 10.0g saturates (50%), 6.9g sugars (8%), 2.59g salt (43%)

Did you know?
The key ingredients in this recipe are the vinegar and soy sauce, which enhance the flavour of the chicken during marinating. In fact, the word 'adobo' is from the Spanish word meaning 'marinade or sauce' and has been used to describe this dish since the 16th century – a time when there was Spanish colonial influence in the Philippines.

Chicken and ale stew

The darker the ale, the richer this dish will be; the brandy deepens the flavour too. Mashed potato is good with this stew

4 chicken breast fillets
by Sainsbury's
30g unsalted butter
2 tbsp vegetable oil
750g onions, thinly sliced
30g plain flour
3–4 tbsp Basics brandy
by Sainsbury's
500g mushrooms, quartered
1 bouquet garni, made by tying
together 5–6 parsley sprigs, 2–3
thyme sprigs and 1 bay leaf

2 tsp juniper berries,
gently crushed
500ml ale
250ml hot chicken stock (made
with 1/2 chicken stock cube and
boiling water)
4 tbsp half-fat crème fraîche
a small bunch of fresh flat-leaf
parsley, finely chopped
750g King Edward potatoes,
cooked and mashed, to serve

1 Season the chicken pieces, to taste. Heat the butter and oil in a large flameproof casserole over a medium-high heat until foaming. Add the chicken, skin-side-down (in batches, if necessary) and cook for about 5 minutes on each side until coloured. Remove, cover and set aside.

2 Reduce the heat to medium, add the onions and cook for about 10 minutes, until soft and well coloured. Sprinkle with the flour and cook, stirring, for 1–2 minutes until the flour is just lightly coloured. Return the chicken to the casserole in a single layer.

3 Add the brandy and bring to the boil for a few minutes, using it to baste the chicken. Add the mushrooms, bouquet garni and crushed juniper berries. Pour in the ale and hot stock, bring to the boil, cover with the lid and simmer for 40–50 minutes, until the chicken is tender when pierced and the juices run clear.

4 Discard the bouquet garni and skim off any excess fat from the surface. Stir in the crème fraîche for the last 15 minutes of cooking. Season to taste, if needed. Sprinkle with the chopped parsley and serve with mashed potato.

Per serving: 3238kJ/775kcal (39%), 42.4g fat (61%), 14.8g saturates (74%), 16.1g sugars (18%), 0.93g salt (16%)

Cook's tip
This dish works really well when cooked in a slow cooker. Follow the same method up to the end of step 3, then once it's been brought to the boil transfer everything to the slow cooker. Cover with the lid and cook on auto/low for 6–8 hours or on high for 3–4 hours. Then return to step 4 of the main recipe.

Chicken and broccoli pasta bake

Make Sunday's roast chicken stretch to Monday night's supper with this delicious, crowd-pleasing pasta bake

300g small dried pasta shapes, such as macaroni or spirali by Sainsbury's
200g small broccoli florets
75g unsalted butter
75g plain flour

500ml semi-skimmed milk
50g mature Cheddar cheese, grated
leftover roast chicken (ideally about 300g), chopped small

50g fresh breadcrumbs from day-old bread
25g Parmesan cheese by Sainsbury's, finely grated

1 Preheat the oven to 200°C/180°C fan/gas 6. Then, cook the pasta according to the pack instructions. A couple of minutes before it is ready, add the broccoli and cook until al dente. Drain the pasta and broccoli and return them to the pan off the heat, cover and set aside.

2 Meanwhile, melt the butter in a small, heavy-based saucepan. Whisk in the flour over a low heat and continue to cook for 2 minutes, whisking constantly, until the mixture bubbles and separates. Take the pan off the heat and whisk in the milk, a little at a time, whisking well between each addition, until it has all been added and the sauce is smooth.

3 Return the pan to the heat and cook, stirring constantly, until the sauce thickens. Reduce the heat to low and continue to cook, stirring occasionally, for 5 minutes. Be sure to whisk into the edges of the saucepan, as this is where the sauce can burn.

4 Add the Cheddar cheese, season to taste and cook for 2 minutes until the cheese has melted and the sauce is smooth, thick and creamy. Pour the sauce over the pasta and broccoli and stir in the chicken, avoiding breaking up the broccoli florets.

5 Turn the mixture out into a 25cm ovenproof dish. Mix the breadcrumbs with the Parmesan and sprinkle over the top.

6 Bake in a preheated oven for 20-25 minutes, until golden on top with crisp breadcrumbs and bubbling around the edges. Rest for at least 5 minutes before serving.

Per serving: 3141kJ/748kcal (37%), 26.9g fat (38%), 15.2g saturates (76%), 10.6g sugars (12%), 0.96g salt (16%)

Cook's tip
If you do not have any leftover chicken, add 2 x 200g tins of tuna in spring water by Sainsbury's to the pasta at the end of step 5 before topping and baking as above.

Middle Eastern chicken pittas

This Palestinian peasant dish, known as musakhan, is traditionally served on a thick bread base, but in this portable street version it's housed inside a pitta bread pocket for a delicious on-the-go snack

2 tbsp olive oil, plus extra
for greasing

a knob of unsalted butter

2 onions, sliced

2-3 garlic cloves, crushed

2-3 chicken breasts, skinned
and cut into thin strips

2 tsp sumac by Sainsbury's

1 tsp ground cinnamon

1 tsp ground allspice

juice of 1 lemon

4 pitta breads, halved to form
8 pockets

a small bunch of fresh flat-leaf
parsley, roughly chopped

6-8 tbsp Greek-style yogurt

1 Preheat the oven to 180°C/160°C fan/gas 4. Lightly grease a baking sheet and set aside.

2 Heat the oil and butter in a large, heavy-based frying pan over a medium heat and stir in the onions. When the onions begin to soften, add the garlic and fry for 4-5 minutes, stirring, until the onions turn golden.

3 Add the chicken and sumac and cook for 2-3 minutes. Next, add the cinnamon, allspice and lemon juice. Continue to cook until the chicken is tender and cooked through, with no pink remaining. Season to taste.

4 Fill the pitta pockets with the hot chicken mixture and place on the baking sheet. Transfer to the oven and toast for about 10 minutes. Spoon a little parsley into each pocket, top with a dollop of yogurt and serve hot with some pickles on the side if you like.

Per serving: 1894kJ/450kcal (23%), 12.7g fat (18%), 3.6g saturates (18%), 8.4g sugars (9%), 0.57g salt (10%)

Zesty roast chicken pieces

A great stand-by recipe when all you have is some chicken
and a few store cupboard essentials

finely grated zest of 1 lemon
finely grated zest of 1 orange
2 tbsp orange juice
2 tbsp olive oil
1 tbsp runny honey
1 tbsp soy sauce reduced
salt by Sainsbury's

2 heaped tbsp chopped herbs,
such as flat-leaf parsley,
coriander, dill or
oregano (optional)
2 x 600g pack of chicken thighs
and drumsticks by Sainsbury's

1 Preheat the oven to 200°C/180°C fan/gas 6.

2 Mix all of the ingredients except the chicken together in a large, shallow container.

3 Add the chicken, turning to coat. Cover and leave in the fridge for at least 2 hours,
but preferably 4 hours if possible.

4 Put the chicken pieces in a large oven tray, spaced well apart and in a single layer.
Roast in a preheated oven for 40-45 minutes, turning occasionally, until golden and
crispy, and cooked through, with no pink remaining. Partner this chicken with a warm
new potato salad (see p226).

Per serving: 2207kJ/527kcal (26%), 25.5g fat (36%), 6.3g saturates (32%), 5.5g
sugars (6%), 0.66g salt (11%)

Get ahead
Freeze the raw chicken in the marinade; it'll
keep for 3 months. Defrost thoroughly before
cooking and pick up from the start of step 3 above.

SERVES 4
PREP 25 minutes
COOK 10–15 minutes,
plus resting

Beef fajitas with tomato salsa and guacamole

A popular Tex-Mex recipe, this dish pairs the flavoursome rump steak with Cajun spices and fresh, tangy sauces

1 tbsp olive oil
4 tsp Cajun spice
500g beef rump, from Sainsbury's meat counter
8 plain tortillas by Sainsbury's
4 tbsp soured cream, to serve

FOR THE SALSA
450g tomatoes, skinned
a handful of coriander leaves, chopped
$\frac{1}{2}$ red onion, finely chopped
1 green chilli, deseeded and finely chopped
juice of $1\frac{1}{2}$ limes

FOR THE GUACAMOLE
2 ripe avocados, halved and stoned
juice of 1 lime
1 tbsp olive oil
1 red onion, finely chopped
1 garlic clove, crushed
1 green chilli, deseeded and finely chopped

1 First make the salsa. Roughly chop the tomatoes, removing the core from around the stem, but not the seeds. Place the tomatoes in a bowl and add the coriander, onion, chilli and lime juice. Season to taste and mix well. Cover and set aside.

2 For the guacamole, scoop the avocado flesh into a small bowl and mash gently with a fork. Add the lime juice, oil, onion, garlic and chilli and mix well. Taste and season, if needed. Cover with cling film, making sure it touches the surface of the guacamole (that stops it turning brown), and set aside in the fridge.

3 Heat a griddle pan over a high heat. Meanwhile, mix the oil and Cajun spice in a small bowl. Rub the beef with the oil mix evenly. Sear for 3–4 minutes on each side for medium; cook for an extra 1–2 minutes on each side if you prefer your steak well done. Remove from the heat and rest for 3–5 minutes in a warm place.

4 Warm the tortillas in a dry frying pan. Cut the steaks into strips and divide the meat between the warmed tortillas. Top with the guacamole and salsa and roll up the tortillas. Serve hot with soured cream on the side.

Per serving: 3963kJ/947kcal (47%), 46.2g fat (66%), 16.5g saturates (83%), 12.3g sugars (14%), 3.24g salt (54%)

SERVES 4
PREP 15 minutes
COOK 2½ hours

Pappardelle ragù

The rich, meaty, slow-simmered sauce also works well with any other long-style pasta, such as spaghetti or tagliatelle

30g unsalted butter

2 tbsp olive oil

105g Italian smoked pancetta by Sainsbury's, diced

1 onion, finely chopped

1 celery stick, finely chopped

1 carrot, peeled and finely chopped

2 garlic cloves, crushed

500g lean beef mince

2 tbsp tomato purée

150ml hot beef stock (made with ½ stock cube and boiling water)

390g carton of chopped tomatoes by Sainsbury's

100ml semi-skimmed milk, warmed

450g dried pappardelle pasta by Sainsbury's

grated Parmesan cheese, to serve

1 Melt the butter with the oil in a deep, heavy-based saucepan and fry the pancetta for 1–2 minutes. Add the onion, celery, carrot and garlic, and continue to fry, stirring occasionally, for 10 minutes, or until softened but not coloured.

2 Stir in the meat, breaking up any clumps, then cook for a further 10 minutes, or until it is evenly coloured, stirring frequently. Stir in the tomato purée, stock and tomatoes, season to taste, then bring to the boil.

3 Reduce the heat to very low, cover the pan and simmer very gently for 1½ hours. Stir occasionally to prevent sticking, adding more stock, if necessary. Stir the milk into the ragù, cover and simmer for a further 30 minutes.

4 Bring a large pan of water to the boil. Cook the pappardelle according to the pack instructions, or until cooked but still firm to the bite. Drain well, spoon the ragù over and serve with freshly grated Parmesan cheese.

Per serving: 2869kJ/687kcal (34%), 39.4g fat (56%), 16.9g saturates (85%), 10.2g sugars (11%), 2.03g salt (34%)

Why not try?
Make a richer sauce for pappardelle alla Bolognese. Cook the vegetables and pancetta as in step 1. Replace half the minced steak with 250g lean pork mince, plus 100g dried macaroni and continue with the recipe as above.

Fiery beef fillet with roasted vegetables

This colourful and wonderfully spiced dish has great flavour combinations

about 2kg beef roasting joint Taste the Difference
6 tbsp rapeseed oil
4 tbsp Madras curry paste by Sainsbury's
4 tbsp Greek-style yogurt
a large handful of coriander leaves, chopped
2 tbsp black peppercorns
4 tbsp cumin seeds
1 tbsp coriander seeds

FOR THE VEGETABLES
2 aubergines, sliced lengthways
4 courgettes, sliced
4 red peppers, deseeded and cut into pieces
1 butternut squash, deseeded and sliced lengthways
4 tbsp Madras curry paste by Sainsbury's
8 tbsp rapeseed oil

FOR THE MINT YOGURT (OPTIONAL)
700g Greek-style yogurt
1 cucumber, peeled, deseeded and finely chopped
2 garlic cloves, crushed
4 tbsp shredded mint leaves

1 Preheat the oven to 200°C/180°C fan/gas 6. Meanwhile, heat a large frying pan over a high heat. Brush the beef with 1 tablespoon of the oil. Add the beef to the pan and colour on all sides. Remove from the heat, cover and leave to cool.

2 Mix the curry paste, yogurt and coriander in a bowl and rub the mixture all over the meat.

3 Using a mortar and pestle, roughly crush the peppercorns, cumin and coriander seeds. Sprinkle the spices over the meat evenly, place it in a roasting tin and drizzle with the remaining oil. Cook in the oven for 45 minutes.

4 Meanwhile, place all the vegetables in a separate roasting tin. Mix the curry paste with the oil. Toss the vegetables in this mix to coat and place the roasting tin below the beef in the oven. Roast in the oven for 30 minutes.

5 Once the beef is cooked to your liking, remove it: for medium, a meat thermometer will read 70°C, while well done will be 80°C. If it needs more time, return it to the oven for 10 minutes at a time and retest with the meat thermometer. Remove the beef from the oven and leave it to rest in a warm place for 20 minutes; meanwhile, keep the vegetables warm.

6 To make the mint yogurt, place all of the ingredients in a serving bowl and mix well.

7 Slice the beef into thick steaks, pour over any juices and serve over the vegetables. It's delicious served with a dollop of the mint yogurt on the side if you like.

Per serving: 3954kJ/949kcal (47%), 59.9g fat (86%), 21.3g saturates (107%), 20.4g sugars (23%), 1.04g salt (17%)

SERVES 4
PREP 20 minutes,
plus marinating
COOK 1 hour 45 minutes–
2 hours 15 minutes

Keralan beef curry

This fabulous curry from the southern Indian state of Kerala uses popular local ingredients, such as coconut, turmeric and curry leaves, to produce a distinctively hot, spicy and aromatic dish

5cm cinnamon stick
12 black peppercorns
6 cloves
1 tbsp fennel seeds
1½ tbsp coriander seeds
6 cardamom seeds from pods
1 tsp ground turmeric
2 x 457g packs of British beef braising steak by Sainsbury's, trimmed and cut into 2.5cm chunks

2.5cm piece of fresh root ginger, peeled and finely grated
4 garlic cloves, finely sliced
2 green chillies, deseeded and finely chopped
20 fresh curry leaves, washed, or 16 dried curry leaves
2 onions, thinly sliced
50g coconut pieces, shredded
4 tbsp sunflower, rapeseed or coconut oil

½ tbsp mustard seeds
a handful of coriander leaves, to garnish
a handful of thinly sliced dried coconut, to garnish

1 Heat a small frying pan over a medium heat. Dry-roast the cinnamon, peppercorns, cloves, fennel seeds, coriander seeds and cardamom seeds in the pan, stirring frequently, until lightly coloured and fragrant. Remove from the heat and leave to cool for 2–3 minutes.

2 Use a mortar and pestle, grind the roasted spices to a fine powder and transfer to a large bowl. Add the turmeric and mix well. Then add the meat, ginger, garlic, chillies, most of the curry leaves (retaining some for step 6) and half the onion. Mix to coat the meat. Cover and leave to chill in the fridge for 1 hour.

3 Preheat the oven to 160°C/140°C fan/gas 3. Meanwhile, transfer the meat and its marinade to a large, flameproof casserole. Add 375ml cold water and bring to the boil. Cover and transfer to the oven for 1½–2 hours, until the beef is tender.

4 Remove the casserole from the oven and place it, uncovered, over a high heat. Bring to the boil and cook until all the liquid has evaporated, stirring constantly to prevent the curry from sticking to the bottom. Remove, cover and set aside.

5 Heat a large non-stick frying pan. Add the coconut and toast for 2–3 minutes, stirring constantly, making sure it does not burn. Add the oil, mustard seeds and remaining onion.

6 Cook for 3–4 minutes, or until the onion is golden. Then add the beef mixture and remaining curry leaves. Stir-fry until the beef has a good colour and looks dry, but glossy. Garnish with some coriander and dried coconut. Why not try serving with naan bread as a change from rice together with mango or lime chutney?

Per serving: 2481kJ/592kcal (30%), 26.3g fat (38%), 9.7g saturates (49%), 6.6g sugars (7%), 0.59g salt (10%)

Beef and kale

Tender beef with robust kale is a winning combination. The chilli hint is subtle but is just enough to add interest to the dish, while the anchovies enrich the slowly cooked sauce

3-4 tbsp olive oil
3 x 457g packs of British beef braising steak by Sainsbury's, cut into bite-sized pieces
1 tsp paprika
1 tbsp plain flour
2 onions, roughly chopped
3 garlic cloves, finely chopped

1 green chilli, deseeded and finely chopped
8 anchovies in olive oil, drained
4 large carrots, peeled and roughly chopped
250ml red wine
900ml hot beef or vegetable stock (made with 1 stock cube and boiling water)

4 large potatoes, peeled and roughly chopped
200g pack of curly kale, stems trimmed and leaves roughly chopped

1 Preheat the oven to 160°C/140°C fan/gas 3.

2 Heat 1 tablespoon of the oil in a large flameproof casserole over a medium heat. Season the meat with paprika then toss in the flour. Add the beef to the casserole (in batches and with extra oil, if necessary) and cook for 5-8 minutes, until coloured all over. Remove with a slotted spoon and set aside.

3 Add the remaining oil to the casserole, add the onions and cook for 3-4 minutes, until soft. Stir in the garlic, chilli and anchovies. Cook for 1 minute then add the carrots and cook for a further 2-3 minutes. Pour in the wine and bring to the boil, stirring and scraping up the bits from the bottom of the dish.

4 Pour in the stock and bring back to the boil, add the meat and potatoes, cover and transfer to a preheated oven for 1¹/₂ hours. Check from time to time that it's not drying out, topping up with a little hot water if needed.

5 Add the kale and cook for a further hour; again check that it doesn't dry out too much. Serve in a warmed bowl.

Per serving: 2895kJ/687kcal (34%), 17.6g fat (25%), 4.7g saturates (24%), 11.2g sugars (12%), 2.13g salt (36%)

Cook's tip
This dish works really well when cooked in a slow cooker. Preheat the slow cooker in step 1 and then follow steps 2 and 3 as above. Then transfer everything to the slow cooker, add 600ml hot beef or vegetable stock (so slightly less than above) followed by the meat and potatoes. Cover with the lid and cook on auto/low for 6–8 hours. Add the kale for the last hour of cooking.

SERVES 8
PREP 20 minutes,
plus chilling
COOK 15-30 minutes,
plus resting

Dry-rubbed steak with chimichurri sauce

Crusty on the outside and juicy on the inside, this sweet and spicy steak is wonderfully paired with a fresh and tart green sauce from Argentina

2 tbsp soft light brown sugar
2 tbsp chopped thyme leaves
1 tsp mustard powder
½ tsp smoked paprika
1.35kg rump steak from
Sainsbury's meat counter

FOR THE CHIMICHURRI SAUCE
12 tbsp olive oil, plus
extra for brushing
2 tbsp lemon juice

3 tbsp red wine vinegar
by Sainsbury's
30g fresh flat-leaf parsley,
roughly chopped
4 tbsp roughly chopped
coriander leaves
2 tbsp roughly chopped
oregano leaves
4 garlic cloves, chopped
2 tsp dried red chilli flakes

1 Place the sugar, thyme, mustard and smoked paprika in a food processor. Season to taste and then grind to a fine powder.

2 Place the steak on a large piece of clingfilm and rub the mixture all over. Wrap tightly in the clingfilm and chill for at least 1 hour; the longer you leave it, the better the taste.

3 For the sauce, place all the ingredients in a large serving bowl and mix well to combine. Cover with clingfilm and chill for at least 1 hour, to allow the flavours to develop.

4 Remove the steak and the sauce from the fridge and bring both to room temperature. Set the barbecue to its highest setting to sear. Brush the steak with a little oil and barbecue on both sides until cooked to your liking: rare 60°C, medium 70°C and well done 80°C; be sure to push the meat thermometer into the thickest part of the meat.

5 Remove the steak from the heat, cover loosely with foil and leave to rest for at least 15 minutes. Cut the steak into thick slices and serve with the chimichurri sauce.

Per serving: 2077kJ/499kcal (25%), 35.4g fat (51%), 10.6g saturates (53%), 6.0g sugars (7%), 0.31g salt (5%)

Easy entertaining
This recipe is easy to scale up to entertain family and friends, and makes an impressive centrepiece, as shown in the photo. You can have a joint of beef from Sainsbury's meat counter cut to the size you require.

Cumin beef tagine

Here the beef is slowly cooked in spices for maximum flavour. Cheaper cuts of meat are ideal for slow cooking

2 tsp ground cumin

2 tbsp plain flour

800g braising steak from Sainsbury's meat counter, cut into 2.5cm cubes

3 tbsp olive oil

1 large onion, chopped

4 garlic cloves, peeled and crushed

1 tsp ground ginger

1 tsp ground cinnamon

¹/₂ tsp cayenne pepper

600ml hot chicken stock (made with 1 stock cube and boiling water)

1 small butternut squash, peeled, deseeded and diced

3 red peppers, deseeded and chopped into strips

a handful of raisins (optional)

1 Preheat the oven to 150°C/130°C fan/gas 2. Mix the cumin and flour together and toss the beef in the spiced mixture so it is evenly coated. Heat the oil in a large flameproof casserole or tagine over a medium-high heat and cook the beef in batches for 10 minutes, until evenly coloured.

2 Reduce the heat, then add the onion, garlic and all the spices, stir well to coat and cook for 2 minutes. Pour over the stock and bring to the boil. Reduce the heat once more, season, cover with the lid and cook in a preheated oven for 1¹/₂ hours.

3 Add the squash and then, 15 minutes later, the peppers and raisins, if using, and cook everything for a further 30 minutes, or until tender. You may need to top up with a little hot water and season to taste. Delicious served with baby roast potatoes, couscous or rice.

Per serving: 1610kJ/383kcal (19%), 2.6g fat (17%), 0.7g saturates (16%), 3.1g sugars (15%), 0.25g salt (18%)

Cook's tip
This dish works really well when cooked in a slow cooker. Preheat the slow cooker, if required, at the beginning of step 1. Follow steps 1 and 2 (using only 450ml of stock) until the mixture has been brought to the boil, then reduce the heat and transfer everything to the slow cooker, season, cover with the lid and cook on auto/low for 6–8 hours, or on high for 3–4 hours. Add the squash, peppers and raisins, if using, for the last hour of cooking. Taste and season if needed. Serve as recommended.

Why slow cook?

Slow cooking is a fantastic cooking method: it's easy, saves you time and money, and produces deeply rich and flavoursome meals whether you use an ordinary casserole or an electric slow cooker

Maximise flavour

When meat is allowed to cook slowly, the gelatine is extracted from the meat and bones, resulting in a flavourful, concentrated sauce. The method is also great for non-meat dishes - slow cooking aromatic vegetables and spices, such as cloves, cinnamon and star anise, allows them to release their distinctive flavours into the sauce.

Save time

Any cooking requires a certain amount of preparation, but with slow cooking this is kept to a minimum. Most of the work takes place early on in the cooking process; once the food is in the casserole, you won't need to keep checking on it until the specified cooking time is up.

Save money

Slow cooking makes economical sense as it transforms cheaper cuts of meat - such as pork shoulder, beef brisket, lamb shoulder and chicken thighs - and inexpensive staples, such as beans and lentils, into great meals. What's more, it's a good way of cooking a big batch of stew, bolognese sauce or curry - ideal for feeding a crowd or for freezing for another day. And if you use an electric slow cooker, you can save money on your power bill, as they use much less electricity than traditional ovens - often only as much as a light bulb!

What is a slow cooker?

An electric slow cooker consists of a sturdy, heatproof outer casing and a removable inner cooking pot. There's a fitted lid so that the heat and flavours cannot escape while the food is cooking. Heat settings are easily controlled: low for all-day or overnight cooking; high is for dishes needing 3-6 hours of cooking.

Adapting recipes for the slow cooker

- It's easy to adapt conventional recipes for the slow cooker. Check the recipe against similar ones suggested in the manufacturer's instructions; if you're at all worried, leave it to cook for longer - a slow cooker won't boil dry as its lid traps all the cooking juices and steam within its pot.
- As a general guide, halve the liquid in the original recipe, as it won't have a chance to evaporate. If you've still too much liquid towards the end of your cooking time, you can remove the lid and cook on high to allow it to evaporate; if you've too little juice you can always top it up later on.
- Make sure all frozen ingredients are thawed and meats are thoroughly defrosted before cooking.
- If a recipe requires milk, cream or soured cream, only add this for the last 30 minutes of cooking. For best results, stir in any cream just before serving.

Tips for slow cooking

1 For maximum flavour, brown meat at the start of cooking and soften vegetables such as onions and garlic by gently frying.

2 Be careful not to over season; salty flavours become concentrated with slow cooking. Season to taste lightly initially, then adjust at the end of cooking, if necessary.

3 Woody herbs, such as rosemary and thyme, are robust enough to add at the start of cooking; add delicate herbs, such as parsley and basil, towards the end of cooking.

4 Peppercorns and seeds, such as cumin, coriander and fennel, are best crushed before adding to the pot, so they release their flavours slowly.

5 For best results, the slow cooker should be between half and two-thirds full when all the ingredients have been added for cooking.

6 Don't open the lid to check on your food – this releases heat and breaks the water seal around the lip of the pot, adding a further 20 minutes to the cooking time.

7 Always add delicate ingredients that don't need much cooking, such as fish and seafood, towards the end of the cooking time.

Thai beef salad

This tangy and vibrant salad is perfect for a midweek taste of Asia on your plate as it's super-quick to make

450g sirloin steak from Sainsbury's meat counter
vegetable oil, for brushing
lime wedges, to serve

FOR THE DRESSING
2 tbsp fish sauce
3 tbsp lime juice
1 large garlic clove, thinly sliced
1 tbsp soy sauce reduced salt by Sainsbury's
2 tsp brown sugar or palm sugar
2 tsp peanuts, toasted and chopped

1 tbsp groundnut oil
2 bird's eye chillies, deseeded and finely chopped

FOR THE SALAD
1 Romaine lettuce heart by Sainsbury's, rinsed, dried and finely sliced
10 cherry tomatoes, halved
3 shallots, finely sliced
4 spring onions, trimmed and sliced diagonally
a handful of fresh coriander leaves, chopped

a small handful fresh mint leaves
½ cucumber, halved, deseeded and sliced diagonally

1 Make the dressing by mixing all the dressing ingredients in a bowl and stirring until the sugar has dissolved completely. Cover and set aside.

2 For the salad, place all the ingredients in a bowl and toss to mix. Cover and set aside.

3 Heat a griddle pan over the highest heat. Brush the beef with oil and season to taste. Sear for 3-4 minutes on each side for medium; cook for an extra 1-2 minutes on each side if you prefer your steak well done.

4 Remove from the heat and leave to rest for about 5 minutes. Cut the steaks into thin slices and add to the salad bowl. Remix the dressing, pour over and toss to coat. Then transfer to a large serving platter and serve with lime wedges.

Per serving: 1717kJ/412kcal (21%), 27.8g fat (40%), 11.6g saturates (58%), 7.3g sugars (8%), 2.29g salt (38%)

Three-bean chilli with beef

The long, slow cooking of this extra-special chilli gives a superb flavour while freeing you up to entertain guests

1 green pepper, deseeded
and roughly chopped
1 red pepper, deseeded
and roughly chopped
1 onion, roughly chopped
1 jalapeño chilli by Sainsbury's
or other mild green chilli,
roughly chopped
2 tbsp olive oil
2 x 390g cartons of chopped
tomatoes by Sainsbury's
325g tin sweetcorn in
water, drained

380g carton of black beans by
Sainsbury's, drained and rinsed
400g tin Basics red kidney
beans by Sainsbury's, drained
and rinsed
410g tin cannellini beans by
Sainsbury's, drained and rinsed
3 garlic cloves, finely chopped
500g beef mince 5% fat
by Sainsbury's
1 tsp dried chilli flakes
1 tbsp chilli powder
1 tbsp ground cumin

TO SERVE
cornbread (see page 290),
50g lighter mature Cheddar
cheese, grated
4 tbsp soured cream Be good to
yourself

1 Put the peppers, onion and jalapeño in a large flameproof casserole with a drizzle of oil. Add the tomatoes, sweetcorn and beans. Stir well to incorporate.

2 In a heavy-based frying pan, heat the remaining oil over a medium heat. Add the garlic and fry for 1 minute. Add the beef and cook, stirring occasionally, for 3–4 minutes, or until coloured all over. Transfer to the casserole and season with the spices.

3 Place the uncovered casserole over a low heat and simmer for 2 hours, stirring occasionally, or until the vegetables are tender. Alternatively, place the dish in an oven preheated to 180°C/160°C fan/gas 4. Season to taste and serve hot with cornbread, grated cheese and soured cream.

Per serving: 2025kJ/482kcal (24%), 16.8g fat (24%), 6.2g saturates (31%), 14.5g sugars (16%), 0.53g salt (9%)

Did you know?

Chilli is the official state dish of Texas (also known as chilli con carne) and was popular with the American frontier settlers of the 19th century. Today, there is much debate about whether it should be made with or without beans. Some purists insist on a simple combination of onions, tomatoes, chillies, spices and meat, but more often canned or dried beans are added too.

Braised oxtail with star anise and clementine

Rich and robust, oxtail makes a change from beef and braising it very slowly tenderises it to the full. Prunes are a tasty addition to a stew as their sweetness and texture complement the meat

2 oxtails, about 1.35kg in total from Sainsbury's meat counter, cut into bite-sized pieces
1 tbsp olive oil
2 red onions, sliced
3 garlic cloves, finely chopped
a pinch of dried chilli flakes
350ml red wine

4 star anise by Sainsbury's
a handful of black peppercorns
1 bay leaf
8 soft prunes, stoned and chopped
900ml hot beef stock (made with 1 beef stock cube and boiling water)

4 clementines or 2 oranges, peeled and sliced into rings
a small bunch of fresh parsley leaves, finely chopped, to garnish
500g cooked pasta, to serve

1 Preheat the oven to 150°C/130°C fan/gas 2. Heat half the oil in a large flameproof casserole over a medium heat, then add the meat in batches and fry for 8-10 minutes, until coloured on all sides. Remove with a slotted spoon, cover and set aside.

2 Heat the remaining oil in the casserole over a medium heat, add the onions and soften for 3-4 minutes. Stir through the garlic and chilli flakes, then pour in the wine and let it simmer for about 5 minutes until slightly reduced. Return the meat to the casserole and add the star anise, peppercorns, bay leaf and prunes. Pour over just enough stock to cover the meat.

3 Bring to the boil, then reduce to a simmer. Add the remaining stock, cover and put in the oven for 3 hours. Check occasionally, topping up with a little hot water if it's drying out.

4 Add the clementines or oranges for the last 30 minutes of cooking and leave the casserole uncovered to allow the liquid to reduce slightly. Stir it occasionally to keep the oxtail moist and coated with the sauce. When it's ready, the meat will fall away from the bone. Remove the bones and discard them together with the bay leaf and star anise. Shred the meat and serve on a bed of pasta, sprinkled with the parsley.

Per serving: 3283kJ/789kcal (40%), 54.0g fat (77%), 17.8g saturates (89%), 8.9g sugars (10%), 1.04g salt (17%)

Cook's tip
This dish works well done in a slow cooker. Follow steps 1 and 2, until the onion and wine mixture is simmering. Then transfer to the slow cooker together with the meat, star anise, peppercorns, bay leaf, prunes and 600ml of stock. Cover with the lid and cook on auto/low for 8 hours. Add the clementines or oranges for the last 30 minutes of cooking and continue as above.

SERVES 6
PREP 15 minutes
COOK 2 hours 40 minutes

Boston baked beans

These beans are cooked to a traditional recipe that dates back to the time of the first settlers in America

300g pancetta, diced
3 x 400g tin cannellini beans by Sainsbury's, drained and rinsed
400ml vegetable stock (made with ½ stock cube and boiling water)
300g onion, diced
3 garlic cloves, chopped
300ml molasses
1 tsp garlic powder
60ml cider vinegar by Sainsbury's
2 tsp mustard powder
1 tsp paprika
20g parsley, chopped, to garnish

1 Preheat the oven to 160°C/140°C fan/gas 3. In a heavy-based pan or flameproof casserole, fry the pancetta over a high heat for 5 minutes on each side. Remove from the pan and set aside.

2 Add one tin of beans followed by the stock and one-third of the onion to the pan, then add one-third of the garlic and top with one-third of the bacon. Repeat the same additions to make two more layers.

3 In a medium bowl, whisk together the molasses, garlic powder, vinegar, mustard powder and paprika, and season to taste. Pour over the bean mixture, then bake, uncovered, in a preheated oven for 2½ hours. Season to taste before serving hot, garnished with parsley.

Per serving: 1801kJ/429kcal (22%), 15.8g fat (23%), 5.4g saturates (27%), 36.9g sugars (41%), 0.28g salt (5%)

Why not try?

Try a brown sugar variation by substituting the molasses with the same amount of runny honey and adding 60g brown sugar and 100g tomato ketchup.

SERVES 10
PREP 20 minutes
COOK 2 hours 5 minutes

Whole glazed gammon

A combination of marmalade and pineapple juice gives this succulent gammon a wonderful sweet, sticky finish, plus it makes an impressive table centrepiece

2kg smoked gammon or ham, bone removed and rolled, available from Sainsbury's meat counter

3 heaped tbsp marmalade

2 tbsp pineapple juice

1 tbsp clear honey

1 heaped tbsp soft light brown sugar

2 tbsp wholegrain mustard

1 Preheat the oven to 160°C/140°C fan/gas 2. Place the gammon, skin-side-up, on a rack in a large roasting tin. Pour water to a depth of 3cm into the tin. Cover tightly with foil and seal to ensure that no steam escapes. Cook in a preheated oven for 1 hour 40 minutes.

2 Meanwhile, put the marmalade, pineapple juice, honey, brown sugar and mustard in a large saucepan over a medium heat. Season to taste and bring to the boil. Then, reduce the heat to a simmer and continue to cook for 5-7 minutes, until thickened.

3 Remove the gammon from the oven and increase the oven temperature to 200°C/180°C fan/gas 6. Remove the skin, leaving a thin layer of the fat. Cut a criss-cross pattern in the fat.

4 Brush some of the glaze from the pan over the gammon. Return to the oven for 25 minutes, brushing with the glaze two or three times, until golden and crispy and the joint is cooked through. Remove from the oven and serve hot. This ham goes wonderfully with some simple mashed potato.

Per serving: 1042kJ/249kcal (13%), 11.7g fat (17%), 3.8g saturates (19%), 8.0g sugars (9%), 3.51g salt (59%)

Pork steaks with a tomato and broad bean sauce

Make the most of the broad bean season with this chunky sauce that's a perfect match for tender pork steaks; out of season, frozen beans also work well

2 x 300g pack of pork steaks by Sainsbury's, trimmed
2 tbsp olive oil
a pinch of dried oregano
1 onion, finely chopped
2 garlic cloves, grated or finely chopped

390g carton of chopped tomatoes by Sainsbury's
125g broad beans (shelled weight)
a handful of fresh flat-leaf parsley, very finely chopped

1 Preheat the oven to 200°C/180°C fan/gas 6. Brush the steaks with 1 tablespoon of the oil and sprinkle over the oregano. Sit the steaks in a roasting tin and roast in a preheated oven for 15 minutes until golden. Cut into one of the steaks with a sharp knife to check they are cooked through.

2 Meanwhile, heat the remaining oil in a frying pan over a low heat and add the onion. Cook for 5 minutes, until soft and translucent, then add the garlic, stirring for a couple of seconds.

3 Tip in the tomatoes, including any juices, and bring to the boil. Reduce the heat slightly and simmer for about 15 minutes. Add the broad beans to the pan and cook for a further 10 minutes, adding a little water if the mixture dries out.

4 Taste the sauce and add more seasoning if needed. Stir through the parsley, divide up the sauce, sit each chop on top of the sauce and serve hot.

Per serving: 1016kJ/242kcal (12%), 9.4g fat (13%), 2.2g saturates (11%), 5.3g sugars (6%), 0.18g salt (3%)

Why not try?
Substitute 125g peas (shelled weight; fresh or frozen) for the broad beans in step 3 for a slightly sweeter sauce.

Sausage tray bake

This all-in-one dish has simple, but great flavours, which work equally well with pork or beef sausages, or why not try gluten-free sausages?

4 waxy potatoes, such as Charlotte, halved lengthways
2 sweet potatoes, peeled and cut into chunks
1 red onion, cut into 6 or 8 wedges through the root
1 red pepper, deseeded and cut into 3cm chunks
8 frozen sausages Be good to yourself, defrosted
2 tbsp olive oil
1 tbsp thyme leaves
2 tsp smoked paprika
75g cherry tomatoes

1 Preheat the oven to 200°C/180°C fan/gas 6.

2 Put the vegetables and sausages in a roasting tray large enough to fit them in a single layer. Drizzle with the oil, sprinkle with the thyme and paprika and season to taste.

3 Toss everything together so it is well coated with the oil and spread it out in a single layer with the sausages evenly spaced between the vegetables.

4 Bake in a preheated oven for 30 minutes. Then, remove the tray from the oven, add the cherry tomatoes, toss everything together and spread out again. Cook for a further 15 minutes, until the sausages are crispy and cooked through, the vegetables are colouring at the edges and the tomatoes have softened.

Per serving: 1617kJ/387kcal (19%), 14.0g fat (27%), 5.5g saturates (28%), 13.1g sugars (15%), 1.60g salt (27%)

Cook's tip
Tray bakes are a great way to accommodate the likes and dislikes of the whole family. Cook a variety of vegetables and everyone can pick the ones they like.

SERVES 8
PREP 30 minutes,
plus chilling
COOK 1 hour 15 minutes,
plus resting

Auvergne tourte

Since the Auvergne region of France is famed for its incredible landscapes, it's no surprise this tart would make a great lunch – warm or cold – to enjoy in the great outdoors

FOR THE FILLING
30g Butterlicious spread by Sainsbury's
1 large onion, finely sliced
1 garlic clove, finely chopped
125g unsmoked bacon medallions Be good to yourself, cubed
650g waxy new potatoes, such as Charlotte or Anya, peeled and finely sliced

100g lighter mature cheese by Sainsbury's, grated
1 tbsp finely chopped flat-leaf parsley
200ml half-fat crème fraîche
1 egg yolk

FOR THE PASTRY
2 x 375g ready-rolled puff pastry by Sainsbury's
plain flour, for dusting
1 egg yolk, beaten with 1 tbsp cold water, for glazing

1 Melt the spread in a large saucepan. Add the onion and cook over a medium heat for 10 minutes. Then, add the garlic and bacon cubes and cook for a further 5 minutes, until the onion is soft but not coloured.

2 Preheat the oven to 180°C/160°C fan/gas 4. Unroll the pastry on a lightly floured work surface and, using a deep 23cm metal pie tin as a template, cut out one circle large enough to top the pie; use the other roll of pastry to line the tin, leaving a 1cm overhang around the edges. Wrap in cling film and chill the base and the top for 20 minutes. Use any pastry leftovers to make some decorations for the top of the pie.

3 Brush the inside of the pastry case, including the edges, with some of the egg yolk mixture. Reserve the remainder.

4 Layer the pastry case with one-third of the potatoes. Cover them with half the onion and bacon mixture and half the cheese. Scatter over half the parsley and season to taste. Repeat the procedure and finish with a final layer of potatoes.

5 Whisk together the crème fraîche and egg yolk, and pour over the pie filling. Top the pie with the pre-cut circle of pastry, pressing it down around the edges to seal. Crimp the edges.

6 Brush the top of the pie with the remaining egg yolk mixture and cut 2 small slits in the top to allow steam to escape. Place the pie on a baking tray and bake for 1 hour, until well cooked, puffed up and golden. Set aside to rest for 15–20 minutes before serving.

Per serving: 2235kJ/534kcal (27%), 26.5g fat (38%), 12.7g saturates (64%), 5.1g sugars (6%), 1.37g salt (23%)

Texas-style ribs with barbecue sauce

This Southern-style American sauce has a dark, sweet, smoky flavour that is hard to resist

3 tbsp sunflower oil

1 large red onion, finely chopped

3 garlic cloves, crushed

180ml tomato ketchup

3 tbsp red wine vinegar

3 tbsp molasses or treacle

$1^1/_2$ tsp Worcestershire sauce

3 tsp smoked paprika

$^3/_4$ tsp cayenne pepper

freshly ground black pepper

8-12 meaty pork spare ribs from Sainsbury's meat counter

1 Heat the oil in a small pan and fry the onion over a medium heat for 5 minutes, until softened. Add the garlic and cook for 1 minute. Add the remaining ingredients, apart from the ribs, with 100ml of water and whisk. Bring the mixture to the boil, reduce the heat to a low simmer and cook, uncovered, for 20 minutes, until it has reduced to a thick sauce. Then, cover and leave to cool.

2 Reserve half of the sauce for serving. Rub the rest into the ribs, cover and leave to marinate in the fridge for at least 2 hours. Near the end of the marinating time, preheat the oven to 200°C/180°C fan/gas 6.

3 Cook the ribs in a baking tray in a preheated oven for 20-25 minutes, turning once, until tender and cooked through. Warm up the remaining sauce thoroughly to serve alongside.

Per serving: 1992kJ/478kcal (24%), 29.7g fat (42%), 9.6g saturates (48%), 22.2g sugars (25%), 0.56g salt (9%)

Get ahead

The cooked, cooled sauce can be frozen for up to 6 months, or make double the recipe and freeze half for another time (you'll need to defrost fully before using).

SERVES 4
PREP 20 minutes
COOK 40 minutes,
plus resting

Mushroom lasagne

This baked lasagne recipe comes from Le Marche in central Italy, where wild mushrooms, including porcini, are plentiful

250g closed cup white or chestnut mushrooms by Sainsbury's or 50g dried porcini, soaked and drained
50g unsalted butter
2 tbsp plain flour
600ml skimmed milk
4 tbsp diced prosciutto cotto

250g wholewheat lasagne sheets by Sainsbury's
2 tbsp olive oil, plus extra for greasing
4 tbsp half-fat crème fraîche
4 tbsp grated Parmesan cheese
1 egg, whisked

1 Clean the mushrooms and wipe over the caps – do not rinse. Depending on the size, slice or dice them. In a heavy-based saucepan, melt half the butter, add the mushrooms and fry until they lose most of their moisture. Remove, cover and set aside.

2 In the same pan, melt the remaining butter, then stir in the flour and fry gently until the mixture looks sandy, but do not let it darken. Gradually whisk in the milk, until you have a smooth sauce. Boil and stir for 10 minutes, until the sauce is thick enough to coat the back of a wooden spoon. Remove a ladleful of the sauce and reserve. Stir the mushrooms and prosciutto into the remaining sauce.

3 Meanwhile, prepare the lasagne according to the pack instructions.

4 Preheat the oven to 180°C/160°C fan/gas 4. Lightly oil the base of a medium-sized gratin dish and line with about one-third of the pasta sheets. Spread with half the mushroom sauce and top with another layer of lasagne. Repeat the layering. Whisk the reserved sauce with crème fraîche, most of the cheese (keeping some back for the top) and egg. Top the pasta with the sauce and sprinkle with the reserved cheese and a trickle of oil. Bake for 10–15 minutes, until the top is golden and the sides are bubbling. Remove from the oven and leave to rest for 5–10 minutes before serving.

Per serving: 2185kJ/522kcal (34%), 23.6g fat (34%), 10.5g saturates (54%), 10.3g sugars (11%), 0.66g salt (11%)

Sauces

It's good to have a handful of sauces in your repertoire, either to rustle up at a moment's notice or to make as a batch and freeze for later use

Bechamel sauce

Also known as white sauce, béchamel is brilliant for pasta dishes, such as lasagnes and macaroni cheese

MAKES 850ml or enough for 2 meals for a family of 4

Put ½ sliced onion, the chopped stalks from a handful of flat-leaf parsley, ½ tsp grated nutmeg, 20 black peppercorns and 850ml whole milk in a large pan, then bring to a simmering point, but take care not to let it boil. Remove from the heat, cover and let it go cold to infuse the flavours. Strain the milk into a clean pan, discarding the onion, peppercorns and parsley, then add 80g unsalted butter and 40g plain flour. Gradually bring to simmering point, whisking continuously to create a smooth sauce. Continue to cook for 5-10 minutes until the sauce has thickened. To freeze, once cooled, transfer to an airtight container or sealable bag and freeze for up to 3 months. Defrost overnight in the fridge and reheat gently, whisking so it doesn't split.

Cheese sauce
Use 300ml of the béchamel sauce (above) and, off the heat, add 75g grated mature Cheddar cheese and 1 tsp mustard (wholegrain or Dijon).

Parsley sauce
Use 300ml of the béchamel sauce and stir in 2 tbsp finely chopped parsley at the end.

Home-made mayonnaise

Get the hand of making the basic recipe and all sorts of flavour combinations become possible as well

MAKES 360ml

Make sure all the ingredients are at room temperature before you start to make the mayonnaise to help prevent curdling. Place 2 egg yolks, 2 tbsp white wine vinegar and 1 tsp Dijon mustard in a food processor and blend for 1-2 minutes, or until the mixture is pale and creamy. With the motor still running, slowly pour in 300ml olive oil in a steady stream through the feeder tube. Blend until thick, creamy and smooth. Spoon into a bowl and stir in the juice of ½ lemon and season to taste. Refrigerate, covered, until needed.

Aïoli
Add 4 crushed garlic cloves to the egg yolks, then continue as above. Serve with crunchy vegetable crudités or fish (see also the lemon aïoli on p54).

Basic tomato sauce

Make this sauce ahead of time and use it as a short cut when cooking pasta dishes, pizzas and bakes

MAKES 1.25 litres or enough for 3 meals for a family of 4

Heat 1 tbsp olive oil in a pan over a medium heat. Add 1 large chopped onion, 2 crushed garlic cloves and 1 tbsp dried oregano, and cook gently, stirring occasionally, until the onion has softened. Tip 4 x 390g cartons chopped tomatoes into the pan and stir gently. Cook the sauce over a low heat for 30 minutes. If you like, blend with a hand-held blender for a super-smooth sauce. When cool, freeze batches of sauce in small containers or freezer bags for up to 6 months and use as required.

Chilli tomato sauce

Add 1 chopped fresh red chilli to 600ml of the tomato sauce (above), including the seeds if you want a very hot sauce; remove the seeds for a milder version.

Home-made tomato ketchup

Make up a batch of this simple tomato ketchup to give the family a home-made treat

MAKES 300ml

Heat ½ tbsp olive oil in a pan, then add 1 large chopped onion and cook for 10 minutes until soft. Tip the onion into a food processor and then add 2 x 390g cartons of chopped tomatoes, 50g light muscovado sugar, 75ml cider vinegar and 1 tsp English mustard powder. Whizz until smooth. Spoon into a pan and cook over a medium-low heat for 1 hour, stirring frequently. Cool and store in the fridge in a sterilised airtight container for up to 2 weeks.

Home-made barbecue sauce

A great partner to a range of barbecue meats and vegetables. Use as a dip or as a sauce for coating chicken for barbecuing

MAKES 350ml

Melt 20g unsalted butter in a pan, then add 1 finely chopped large onion and cook until soft. Add 300g tomato ketchup by Sainsbury's, 75ml orange juice, 2 tbsp maple syrup, 2 tbsp dark muscovado sugar and 2 tbsp Worcestershire sauce and cook over a medium-low heat for 45 minutes, stirring frequently, until the sauce has reduced and thickened. Cool and store the sauce in an airtight container in the fridge for up to 2 weeks.

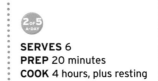
Bavarian roast pork

This German favourite features caraway seeds, which introduces
a delicate aniseed flavour, blending with the garlic

1.8kg skin-on boneless pork
shoulder from Sainbury's
meat counter
2 tbsp caraway seeds
1 tbsp paprika
4 tbsp olive oil
500g white onions, chopped
500g carrots, peeled and
cut into chunks

500g waxy potatoes, such
as Charlotte or Anya, peeled
and cut into chunks
4 garlic cloves
250ml vegetable stock (made
with ½ stock cube and boiling
water; optional)

1 Preheat the oven to 160°C/140°C fan/gas 3. Use a knife to lightly score the skin of the
pork. Combine the caraway seeds, paprika and half the oil in a bowl; season to taste. Coat
the meat with two-thirds of the spice mixture.

2 Place the onion, carrots, potatoes and garlic in a roasting tin and toss with the remaining
oil and spice mix. Place the pork in the pan fat-side-uppermost.

3 Roast the pork and vegetables in the oven for 3–4 hours, or until the internal
temperature of the meat reaches 75–80°C. Add stock to the roasting tin to prevent the
vegetables from drying out, if required.

4 Remove from the oven, leave to rest for at least 10 minutes before carving and serve
alongside the roasted vegetables.

Per serving: 3700kJ/886kcal (44%), 48.7g fat (70%), 15.7g saturates (79%),
13.2g sugars (15%), 1.17g salt (20%)

Why not try?
Use the top rump of beef in place of the pork
shoulder. For the marinade, use 1 tbsp ground
allspice instead of the caraway seeds and 1 tbsp
chipotle chilli paste by Sainsbury's instead of the
paprika. Cook as per the recipe above and serve
with the roasted vegetables.

Pork tenderloin with apple gravy

This updated version of the dinner party classic is family friendly as it uses apple juice instead of wine

2 tbsp plain flour
450g piece of pork tenderloin by Sainsbury's, sliced into 2cm pieces
1 tbsp olive oil
2 tbsp unsalted butter
150ml apple juice

150ml hot chicken stock (made with ½ stock cube and boiling water)
4 tbsp single cream
1 tbsp finely chopped sage leaves

TO SERVE
300g pack of dwarf green beans
750g Maris Piper potatoes
1 tbsp olive oil
few leaves from 1 sprig of fresh rosemary (optional)

1 Preheat the oven to 200°C/180°C fan/gas 6 for cooking the potatoes. Meanwhile, cut the potatoes into cubes and toss in the olive oil and add the rosemary, if using. Roast the potatoes in the oven for 35-40 minutes.

2 When the potatoes are nearly cooked, place 1 tablespoon of the flour on a plate and season to taste. Toss the meat in it, lightly coating all sides, and shake off any excess flour. Turn down the oven temperature to 130°C/110°C fan/gas ½ to keep the potatoes warm and later on the cooked pork.

3 Heat the olive oil and 1 tablespoon of the butter in a large, deep-sided frying pan. Sear the pork pieces a few at a time for 2-3 minutes on each side until well coloured. Work in batches, as the pan must not be crowded or the meat will fail to form a good crust. Keep the cooked pork warm, loosely covered with foil, in the oven.

4 Heat the remaining tablespoon of butter in the pan and whisk in the remaining flour. Then, whisk in the apple juice and stock, a little at a time, and bring to the boil. Reduce the heat to a simmer and continue to cook and reduce the sauce until it is about half its original volume, then add the cream along with the chopped sage and continue to cook until the sauce is thick and creamy. Season to taste.

5 Return the meat to the pan with any juices that have come from it, and cook for a further minute or 2 until the pork is piping hot once more and cooked through, and the sauce is evenly glossy. Serve with the roasted potatoes and some cooked green beans.

Per serving: 1949kJ/464kcal (23%), 16.6g fat (24%), 7.4g saturates (37%), 7.2g sugars (8%), 0.8g salt (13%)

Why not try?
Use a little leftover white wine or cider in place of the apple juice here, they will enrich the flavours of the sauce.

SERVES 12
PREP 15 minutes
COOK 25 minutes

Bacon and sundried tomato puffs

This summer version of 'toad in the hole' is made more elegant by creating individual servings

2 tbsp olive oil

1 onion, sliced

8 rashers bacon, chopped

150g plain flour

3 eggs, beaten

300ml semi-skimmed milk

4 sundried tomatoes by Sainsbury's, chopped

1 Preheat the oven to 220°C/200°C fan/gas 7. Brush all over a 12-hole muffin tin with the oil.

2 Divide the onion and bacon between the holes and place in a preheated oven for 5 minutes, until starting to colour.

3 Meanwhile, beat together the flour and eggs until smooth; season to taste. Then gradually beat in the milk. You can also do this in a food processor, if you prefer. Stir in the sundried tomatoes and pour into a large jug. Remove the muffin tin from the oven then pour a little batter over the bacon mixture in each of the holes, using up all the batter. Return to the oven and bake in a preheated ove for 15-20 minutes, or until puffed and golden. Serve straightaway.

Per serving: 625kJ/149kcal (8%), 7.7g fat (11%), 2.4g saturates (12%), 2.5g sugars (3%), 0.55g salt (9%)

Cook's tip
Make a large family-style bake by cooking the bacon and onion in a 20cm x 30cm roasting tin. Pour over the batter and return to the oven for 35–40 minutes, until puffed and golden.

SERVES 8
PREP 30 minutes,
plus cooling and marinating
COOK 3 hours, plus resting

Slow-cooked shoulder of pork

Also known as pulled pork, this joint is cooked until it falls apart juicily, shredded, then is smothered in a delicious sauce

1 tbsp sunflower oil, plus extra for rubbing
1 onion, finely chopped
2 garlic cloves, crushed
100ml tomato ketchup
4 tbsp cider vinegar by Sainsbury's

1 tsp hot pepper sauce
1 tsp Worcestershire sauce
1 tsp dried mustard powder
2 tbsp runny honey
2kg bone-in pork shoulder from Sainsbury's meat counter

TO SERVE
2 x 8 tortilla wrap packs
150g reduced-fat soured cream
230g tomato salsa
3 x 170g bags of rocket leaves by Sainsbury's
1 red onion, finely sliced

1 Heat the oil in a small, heavy-based pan. Fry the onion over a medium heat for 5 minutes, until softened. Add the garlic and cook for 1 minute. Add the remaining ingredients, apart from the pork, along with 100ml water and whisk well.

2 Bring to the boil, reduce the heat to a simmer and cook, uncovered, for 20 minutes, until reduced to a thick sauce. Cool, then use a hand blender or food processor to blend it until smooth.

3 Rub the pork with the sauce, cover and allow to marinate in the fridge for at least 4 hours, but preferably overnight.

4 Preheat the oven to 180°C/160°C fan/gas 4. Put the pork and marinade in an oven tray just big enough to fit it. Put a piece of greaseproof paper over the top (to stop the skin sticking to the foil) and seal with a double layer of foil. Cook the pork for 2½ hours.

5 Prepare a barbecue for cooking. Remove the meat from the oven. Pat the skin dry with kitchen paper and rub in a little oil, and season to taste. Grill it over a hot barbecue for 10-15 minutes on each side, skin-side-down first; carefully turn with tongs, but do not turn it until the crackling is crispy.

6 Meanwhile, pour the juices from the oven tray into a saucepan and first pour, then skim off all the fat. Reduce the sauce over a medium heat to a thick pouring consistency.

7 Cut the crackling off the meat and leave it uncovered (or it will go soft) while you rest the meat wrapped in foil for 10 minutes. When ready to serve, cut the crackling into small shards and use sparingly. Shred the pork into a juicy pile, pour over the sauce and serve with the wraps and all the trimmings.

Per serving: 3212kJ/766kcal (38%), 31.1g fat (44%), 10.6g saturates (53%), 15.1g sugars (17%), 1.8g salt (30%)

Pork with fennel and mustard

The soft and sweet aniseed notes of the fennel marry well with the pork. Serve this dish with some soft bread to soak up all the wonderful juices and sauce

3 tbsp olive oil
1 large onion, sliced
2 small fennel bulbs, sliced
550g lean pork medallions from Sainsbury's meat counter, cut into bite-sized pieces
4 garlic cloves, finely chopped
75ml dry white wine

1 tbsp wholegrain mustard
$1/2$ tsp paprika
a small handful of fresh flat-leaf parsley, chopped
$1/2$ tbsp chopped sage leaves
$1/2$ tbsp chopped rosemary leaves
1 tbsp plain flour
450ml semi-skimmed milk

1 Preheat the oven to 180°C/160°C fan/gas 4. Heat the oil in a large heavy-based pan, add the onion and fennel and cook for 5 minutes, or until the vegetables begin to soften. Add the pork and cook, stirring occasionally, for 5 minutes, or until no pink remains. Add the garlic and cook for 1 minute, then stir in the wine and mustard, raise the heat and allow to boil for 3 minutes while the alcohol evaporates.

2 Next, stir in the paprika and the chopped herbs, then add the flour and mix well. Add a little of the milk, mix to a smooth paste, then stir in the rest of the milk. Season to taste and cook for 5 minutes, adding a little more milk if the mixture looks dry.

3 Transfer the contents of the pan to a casserole dish, cover and cook in a preheated oven for 25 minutes, or until piping hot and serve.

Per serving: 1423kJ/340kcal (17%), 15.4g fat (22%), 3.9g saturates (20%), 9.1g sugars (10%), 0.61g salt (10%)

Why not try?
Adapt this recipe for a delicious beef dish with celery and mustard. Prepare in exactly the same way, but use 2 celery hearts, sliced, instead of the fennel and 500g beef frying steak, cut in thin strips, instead of the pork. Substitute 2 tsp chopped fresh thyme instead of the sage.

Sweet chilli pork sausage and tomato skewers

Cherry tomatoes are ideal for skewers, as they hold their shape far more successfully than quartered or halved larger tomatoes. Team them with slices from a chorizo ring, chorizo-style pork sausages or beef and cracked black pepper sausages

8 pork and sweet chilli sausages by Sainsbury's, cut into large pieces
12 cherry tomatoes
a few bay leaves

a little olive oil, for brushing
a large sprig of fresh rosemary, leaves picked and finely chopped

TO SERVE
2 x 170g bags of Italian-style salad by Sainsbury's, to serve
½ tbsp olive oil

1 If you are using wooden or bamboo skewers, soak them in cold water for 30 minutes first, to avoid them burning on the grill.

2 Thread the sausages and cherry tomatoes alternately onto the skewers, interspersing them occasionally with the bay leaves. Brush each sausage and tomato skewer with oil, sprinkle over the chopped rosemary leaves and season to taste.

3 Heat a barbecue, ridged cast-iron grill pan or griddle until hot. Add the skewers and grill for 5-8 minutes on each side, until the sausages are cooked through. Serve with the salad lightly dressed with the oil.

Per serving: 1527kJ/367kcal (18%), 23.8g fat (34%), 7.8g saturates (39%), 6.8g sugars (8%), 1.75g salt (29%)

Why not try?

A delicious alternative is pork and apricot skewers. Cut 350g pork fillets in 2.5cm chunks. Add 8 cherry tomatoes and 4 halved and stoned apricots. Toss in 2 tbsp olive oil mixed with 1 crushed garlic clove, 1 tsp smoked paprika, 1 tsp ground cinnamon and season to taste. Marinate for 2 hours. Thread alternately on to skewers with a few bay leaves. Grill as before, brushing with any remaining marinade until the pork is cooked through.

Forfar bridies

A traditional Scottish pie, ideal for sharing when out and about on the hills, at a football match or at a picnic

2 x 375g ready-rolled shortcrust pastry by Sainsbury's
plain flour, for dusting

FOR THE FILLING
1 x 500g pack of lamb mince
20% fat by Sainsbury's
75g light vegetable suet, grated
1 onion, finely chopped
1 tbsp chopped flat-leaf parsley

1 Preheat the oven to 200ºC/180ºC fan/gas 6. For the filling, place all the ingredients in a large bowl and mix well to combine.

2 Remove the pastry from the fridge and, on a lightly floured surface, cut 4 round or oval shapes; it may be easier to cut them round and roll them into ovals. Place one-quarter of the meat mixture onto one side of each pastry oval, leaving a border at the edges.

3 Moisten the edges of the pastry ovals with water. Fold the pastry over to enclose the filling and crimp the edges with a fork to neaten and seal. Make a small hole on the top of each pie to allow steam to escape and chill for 1 hour.

4 Transfer to a baking tin and bake in a preheated oven for 40 minutes. These pies can be served warm or cold; each bridie serves 2 so perfect for sharing.

Per serving: 2614kJ/628kcal (31%), 38.9g fat (56%), 19.7g saturates (90%), 1.8g sugars (2%), 0.5g salt (8%)

Why not try?
Try using minced beef in place of lamb, or marjoram in place of parsley. Add 1 tsp of mustard to the filling and cook the pies as above.

Bulgar wheat with lamb and chickpeas

The classic combination of chickpeas and lamb makes a filling supper dish, while the bulgar wheat adds a light, nutty flavour

plain flour, for dusting
450g lean lamb by Sainsbury's, cut into bite-sized pieces
2 tbsp vegetable oil
125g frozen peas
1 onion, finely chopped
1 tbsp chopped thyme leaves
2 x 400g tins chickpeas by Sainsbury's, drained and rinsed

1.2 litres vegetable stock (made with 2 stock cubes and boiling water)
275g bulgar wheat
1 tbsp finely chopped dill fronds, plus extra to garnish

1 Dust the meat with flour until coated. Cook the meat in batches: heat 1 tablespoon of the oil in a large frying pan, add some of the meat and cook until golden. Repeat for the rest of the meat. Remove the meat with a slotted spoon, cover and set aside.

2 Tip the peas into a bowl of boiling water, leave for few minutes, then drain and refresh with cold water, cover and set aside.

3 Heat 1 tablespoon of oil in the pan, add the onion and cook for 5 minutes, or until soft and transparent. Stir in the thyme. Return the meat to the pan along with the chickpeas. Increase the heat, add a little of the stock and bring to the boil. Reduce to a simmer and then add most of the remaining stock, reserving 300ml (to cook the couscous). Continue to cook over a low heat for about 20 minutes, or until the liquid thickens and the lamb is cooked through; add more water if necessary.

4 Meanwhile, tip the bulgar wheat into a bowl, pour in the reserved stock, cover with a clean tea towel and leave for 8-10 minutes. Fluff up with a fork, stir in the peas and dill and season to taste. Serve with the lamb mixture on top and a garnish of dill.

Per serving: 1422kJ/338kcal (17%), 9.6g fat (14%), 2.1g saturates (11%), 3.1g sugars (3%), 1.34g salt (22%)

Lamb stifado

Roasting lamb is popular during Easter in Greece. The super-slow cooking makes the meat incredibly succulent and tender

1.35kg leg of lamb from
Sainsbury's meat counter
2 tbsp olive oil
3 garlic cloves, crushed
1 tsp ground cinnamon
1 tsp dried thyme

1 tsp dried oregano or marjoram
juice of 1 lemon
1 onion, sliced into rings
2 carrots, peeled and halved
lengthways
2 tbsp chopped flat-leaf parsley

1 Preheat the oven to 150°C/130°C fan/gas 2. Place the lamb in a roasting tin. In a small bowl, mix the oil, garlic, cinnamon and herbs together and brush over the lamb. Sprinkle with the lemon juice and season to taste.

2 Half-fill the tin with water, add the onion and carrots. Cook in a preheated oven for 3 hours, basting every 30 minutes and topping up with more water if necessary.

3 Cover with a large piece of foil and cook for a further 1½-2 hours, or until the meat comes away from the bone.

4 Remove from the oven and leave to rest for 20 minutes, covered with foil. Arrange the lamb and vegetables on a platter, scatter the parsley over and serve.

Per serving: 1681kJ/404kcal (20%), 26.1g fat (37%), 9.8g saturates (49%), 6.2g sugars (7%), 0.28g salt (5%)

Lamb chops Champvallon

Legend has it that one of Louis XIV's mistresses created this delicious dish, which sandwiches chops between layers of sliced potatoes and onions, in an attempt to stay in the king's good books

1 tbsp olive oil

6-8 lamb loin chops, each 2.5cm thick, (total weight about 1kg) from Sainsbury's meat counter, trimmed of any excess fat

4 onions, thinly sliced

1.1kg baking potatoes, peeled and very thinly sliced

a small bunch of fresh thyme, leaves chopped, plus a few sprigs, to serve

3 garlic cloves, finely chopped

1 litre hot vegetable stock (made with 1 stock cube and boiling water)

1 Preheat the oven to 180°C/160°C fan/gas 4. Heat the oil in a large flameproof casserole over a high heat. Add the chops and cook for 1-2 minutes on each side, until well coloured. Remove from the casserole, cover and set aside.

2 Pour off all but about 1 tablespoon of fat from the casserole. Add the onions and cook over a medium heat for 3-4 minutes, until soft. Transfer to a large bowl.

3 Gently stir the potato slices and thyme leaves into the softened onions and season to taste. Brush a 23cm x 32cm baking dish with oil. Spread half the potato mixture on the dish; then sprinkle with the garlic. Arrange the chops on top. Cover with the remaining potato, arranging the slices neatly in rows. Pour over enough stock to come just to the top of the potatoes and season to taste. Bake uncovered for 2 hours, or until the lamb and potatoes are tender when pierced. Serve the chops, potatoes and onion with a spoonful of the cooking liquid, garnished with sprigs of thyme.

Per serving: 3740kJ/888kcal (44%), 24.0g fat (34%), 9.9g saturates (50%), 12.7g sugars (14%), 1.36g salt (23%)

Cook's tip
You can cook this dish in a slow cooker. Preheat the slow cooker at the beginning of step 1 and then follow the method until the potatoes have been added to the onion and herb mixture in step 3. Spread half the potato mixture at the bottom of the slow cooker, then sprinkle with the garlic. Arrange the chops on top. Cover with the remaining potato, arranging the slices neatly in rows. Pour over enough stock to come just to the top of the potatoes (about 600ml). Cover with the lid and cook on auto/low for 6–8 hours. Serve as above.

Rack of lamb with celeriac galettes

This dish makes for easy entertaining and involves no carving. Here, celeriac partners with potatoes to make an impressive galette, which works marvellously with the lamb

30g unsalted butter, plus an extra knob of butter

1 small onion, chopped

1 carrot, peeled and finely chopped

2 streaky bacon rashers, chopped

1 garlic clove, crushed

300ml red wine

1 tbsp tomato purée by Sainsbury's

1 tbsp chopped flat-leaf parsley

300ml hot lamb stock (made with ½ stock cube and boiling water)

1 tbsp redcurrant jelly

1 tbsp rapeseed oil

2 x 300g packs of lamb rack by Sainsbury's, cut in half to make each piece 3 ribs

FOR THE GALETTES

300g waxy potatoes, such as Charlotte, thinly sliced

1 celeriac, peeled and thinly sliced

25g unsalted butter, melted

freshly ground white pepper

1 tbsp chopped rosemary leaves

1 Preheat the oven to 180°C/160°C fan/gas 4 and line a baking sheet with baking parchment. For the galettes, place the potato and celeriac in a large bowl. Pour the melted butter over, season to taste and sprinkle over the rosemary.

2 Arrange the celeriac slices on the baking sheet to create 4 overlapping disc-like shapes, roughly 12cm in diameter. Place the potato in neat overlapping circles over each disc. Make sure the galettes are spaced out evenly to avoid sticking to each other during cooking. Bake for 40-45 minutes, until tender.

3 Meanwhile, heat half the butter in a heavy-based pan. Sauté the onion, carrot, bacon and garlic for 2 minutes, until soft. Add the wine, tomato purée and parsley and cook for 5-10 minutes to reduce by half. Add the stock and jelly and cook for 5 minutes to reduce by a third. Strain, return to the pan, beat in the remaining butter and season to taste.

4 Once the galettes are out of the oven, increase the temperature to 200°C/180°C fan/gas 6. Heat the oil and the knob of butter in a ovenproof frying pan. Add the racks and fry for about 5 minutes, until well coloured on both sides. Season to taste and cook in the oven for 10-15 minutes or until the meat is cooked through. To serve, place the lamb on top of one of each of the potato and celeriac galettes and drizzle over the cooking juices.

Per serving: 2534kJ/611kcal (31%), 41.8g fat (60%), 14.6g saturates (48%), 10.0g sugars (11%), 1.33g salt (22%)

Greek lamb pasta bake

This dish, known as pastitsio makaronia, offers a pasta alternative to the aubergine-based moussaka and is similar to lasagne

350g dried tubular pasta, such as penne, rigatoni or macaroni

olive oil or unsalted butter, for drizzling and greasing

2 tbsp grated lighter mature cheese by Sainsbury's

FOR THE MEAT SAUCE

2-3 tbsp olive oil

2 medium onions, chopped

2-3 garlic cloves, chopped

500g minced lamb (you could use beef instead)

1 glass red wine

500g of fresh or tinned tomatoes, skinned and chopped, or a mixture of the two

2 tbsp tomato purée by Sainsbury's

1-2 bay leaves

a short cinnamon stick

FOR THE TOPPING

600ml skimmed milk

2 eggs, plus 1 yolk

2 tbsp grated lighter mature cheese by Sainsbury's, plus 2 tbsp extra to garnish

freshly grated nutmeg

2-3 tbsp fresh breadcrumbs

1 For the meat sauce, heat the oil in a large pan and gently fry the onions and garlic until soft, but without colour. Add the meat and mash into the hot juices until no pink remains. Add the wine and boil for 1-2 minutes, until the steam no longer smells of alcohol. Add the tomatoes, tomato purée, bay leaves and cinnamon, and simmer gently for 30 minutes, until the meat is tender and the sauce reduced. Season to taste, cover and set aside.

2 Cook the pasta according to the pack instructions, until al dente. Drain, toss with a little oil and cheese, cover and set aside.

3 For the topping, whisk the milk with the eggs, hard cheese and nutmeg. Set aside.

4 Preheat the oven to 180°C/160°C fan/gas 4. Grease the base of a 25cm x 25cm gratin dish and spread around half the pasta. Remove and discard both the bay leaf and the cinnamon stick from the meat sauce.

5 Cover the pasta with the meat sauce and top with the remaining pasta, smoothing into the corners and patting it down. Drizzle over the milk-egg mixture.

6 Bake in a preheated oven for 30-45 minutes, until the top is firm and golden. Sprinkle with the cheese mixed with the breadcrumbs, a drizzle of oil and slip under a hot grill to bubble and colour the top. Serve immediately.

Per serving: 2755kJ/657kcal (33%), 29.6g fat (42%), 12.1g saturates (61%), 13.7g sugars (15%), 0.8g salt (13%)

Minced lamb with squash and green chillies

An excellent combination, the minced meat benefits from the long, slow cooking and stirring mint and oregano leaves into the dish adds a distinct freshness

2 tbsp olive oil
1 butternut squash, peeled, deseeded
and chopped into bite-sized pieces
1 onion, finely chopped
a handful of fresh oregano leaves only,
or 1 tsp dried oregano
a handful of fresh thyme, leaves only
3 garlic cloves, finely chopped
1 green chilli, deseeded and finely chopped
450g lamb mince
900ml hot vegetable stock (made with 1 stock
cube and boiling water)

390g carton of chopped tomatoes by Sainsbury's
60g sultanas
a bunch of fresh mint leaves, finely chopped
1-2 tsp harissa paste by Sainsbury's, depending
on how spicy you like it

TO SERVE
360g basmati rice
2 x 200g bags of family sized mixed green salad

1 Preheat the oven to 180°C/160°C fan/gas 4. Heat half the oil in a large flameproof casserole over a medium heat and add the squash cubes. Season to taste and cook for 5-8 minutes, stirring, until the squash starts to turn golden. Remove the squash from the casserole, cover and set aside.

2 Heat the remaining oil in the casserole, add the onion, and cook for 3-4 minutes, until soft. Stir through the oregano, thyme, garlic and chilli and cook for a few more minutes. Add the lamb mince, increase the heat a little and cook, stirring, for 5-8 minutes, until no pink remains. Reduce the heat, return the squash to the casserole, add the stock and tomatoes and bring to the boil. Reduce to a simmer, stir through the sultanas, cover with the lid and put in the oven for 1-1¹/₂ hours. Check occasionally that it's not drying out, topping up with a little hot water if needed. Meanwhile, cook the rice according to the pack instructions.

3 Taste and season, if necessary, then stir through the chopped mint and harissa paste. Serve with basmati rice and a lightly dressed crisp green salad.

Per serving: 2365kJ/563kcal (28%), 20.5g fat (29%), 8.8g saturates (44%), 15.0g sugars (17%), 0.91g salt (15%)

Cook's tip
If you prefer, you can cook this dish in a slow cooker. Follow steps 1 and 2, using 600ml of stock, until the point when the mince and squash mixture has been brought to the boil. Transfer everything to the slow cooker and stir in the sultanas. Cover with the lid and cook on auto/low for 8 hours. Then follow step 3 as above.

Vegetarian

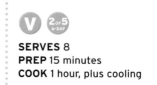

SERVES 8
PREP 15 minutes
COOK 1 hour, plus cooling

Squash, thyme and goat's cheese tart

Perfect for a relaxed weekend lunch with friends, the tangy goat's cheese is a great contrast to the creamy, buttery squash

375g ready-rolled light shortcrust pastry by Sainsbury's
plain flour, for dusting
2 eggs, lightly beaten
1 tbsp olive oil
1 onion, finely chopped

2 garlic cloves, grated or finely chopped
1kg butternut squash, peeled, deseeded and chopped into small cubes
a few sprigs of fresh thyme, leaves picked

120g French goat's cheese Taste the Difference
150ml half-fat crème fraîche
3 x 170g bags of Watercress, spinach and rocket leaves by Sainsbury's

1 Preheat the oven to 200°C/180°C fan/gas 6. Meanwhile, lay out the pastry on a lightly floured work surface and roll, if necessary, to a large circle about 3mm thick; use this pastry to line a 20cm round loose-bottomed fluted tart tin, pressing it into the corners. Trim away the excess and prick the bottom all over with a fork. Line the pastry shell with greaseproof & non-stick baking paper by Sainsbury's and fill the base with baking beans.

2 Bake the pastry shell in the oven for about 15-20 minutes, until the edges of the pastry are golden. Remove the tart tin from the oven, remove the beans and paper. Brush the bottom of the pastry shell with a little beaten egg and return to the oven for 2-3 minutes to crisp.

3 Remove from the oven once again and set aside. Reduce the oven temperature to 180°C/160°C fan/gas 4.

4 Meanwhile, heat the oil in a large frying pan over a low heat. Add the onion and cook gently for about 5 minutes, until soft and translucent. Add the garlic, squash and half of the thyme leaves. Continue cooking over a low heat for 10-15 minutes, until the squash softens and begins to turn golden. You may have to add a little more oil.

5 Spoon the squash and onion mixture into the pastry shell, then crumble the goat's cheese on top. Mix the crème fraîche with the remaining beaten egg. Pour the creamy mixture over the tart filling, then sprinkle with the remaining thyme leaves. Bake in the oven for 20-25 minutes, until the tart is puffed and set. Leave to cool for at least 10 minutes before releasing it from the tin. Serve the tart warm with a rocket salad.

Per serving: 1538kJ/368kcal (18%), 19.8g fat (28%), 10.3g saturates (52%), 6.9g sugars (8%), 0.61g salt (10%)

Cook's tip
Transform any leftover pastry and goat's cheese into some tasty savoury cheese spirals, using a similar method as shown on p10.

Rocket pesto

Rocket is one of the fastest-growing salad crops. Use up any extra by making batches of this pesto sauce and freezing it in ice cube trays to be used as and when you need it

100g pine nuts by Sainsbury's
100g rocket leaves, washed
20g fresh basil leaves (optional)
2 small garlic cloves, crushed
60g Basics Italian hard cheese
by Sainsbury's, grated

freshly ground black pepper
150ml extra virgin olive oil
250g cooked pasta, to serve

1 In a dry frying pan, over a low heat, gently toast the pine nuts for 2–3 minutes, moving them all the time, until they are golden all over. Set aside to cool.

2 Put the rocket and basil leaves, if you're using them, with the cooled pine nuts, garlic, cheese and a good grinding of pepper into a food processor. Add 2–3 tablespoons of the oil and process to a thick paste. If you are serving it with pasta, you can add a little more garlic and cheese, but use less if you are using it as an accompaniment to grilled chicken or fish.

3 Reduce the processor speed and continue to add the oil, in a thin stream, until the pesto becomes a thin paste. Taste and adjust the seasoning if needed. If you prefer a coarser texture, pulse in the food processor until you reach the desired consistency. Serve on warmed plates mixed into cooked pasta, such as pappardelle.

Per serving: 1296kJ/309kcal (16%), 12.0g fat (17%), 2.1g saturates (11%), 0.9g sugars (1%), 0.11g salt (2%)

Why not try?

Use blanched almonds in place of the pine nuts and Sainsbury's creamy blue vegetarian cheese (crumbled or diced) instead of the Italian hard cheese for a more piquant pesto. Follow the recipe above but omit the basil leaves.

SERVES 4 (as a starter)
PREP 10 minutes,
plus marinating
COOK 5-10 minutes

Grilled halloumi salad

Halloumi, a Cypriot cheese traditionally made with sheep's milk but now also made with a mixture of sheep's, goat's and cow's milk, is delicious served warm. Work quickly while preparing the dish, as halloumi hardens on cooling

225g light Cypriot halloumi cheese, cut into 8 slices
finely grated zest and juice of 1 lime
2 tbsp extra virgin olive oil
1 red chilli, deseeded and finely chopped (optional)
freshly ground black pepper
50g Greek pitted Kalamata olives by Sainsbury's
8 cherry tomatoes, halved

2 tbsp coriander leaves, chopped
2 tbsp flat-leaf parsley leaves, chopped
20g pine nuts, toasted
2 x 110g bags of wild rocket leaves by Sainsbury's, washed
100g pomegranate seeds
4 pitta breads, warmed, to serve

1 Place the cheese slices in a single layer in a shallow dish. Evenly sprinkle over the lime zest and juice, oil, chilli, if using, and a good grinding of pepper; turn the cheese slices to coat them evenly. Cover and set aside to marinate for 30 minutes at room temperature.

2 Meanwhile, place the remaining ingredients (all except the pomegranate seeds and pitta bread) in a large bowl and toss to combine. Divide the salad between four plates and then preheat the grill on its highest setting.

3 Line a baking tray with foil. Using a slotted spoon, remove the cheese from the marinade (reserve the marinade) and place on the tray. Grill for 3-5 minutes on each side, turning carefully, until golden. The cheese will not melt, but should soften slightly.

4 Top each plate of salad with two slices of grilled halloumi and scatter over the pomegranate seeds. Drizzle the reserved marinade evenly over each portion, to act as a dressing, and serve with warmed pitta bread.

Per serving: 1911kJ/457kcal (23%), 21.7g fat (31%), 7.1g saturates (36%), 8.1g sugars (9%), 2.62g salt (44%)

Did you know?
First developed in Cyprus in the 4th century, this cheese is popular throughout the eastern Mediterranean and is traditionally wrapped in mint leaves. The dried mint included in the Sainsbury's version maintains a hint of the traditional taste.

Chickpea masala

These spicy chickpeas are traditionally served with a puffed, fried bread called bhatura. It tastes good with any spiced dish and makes a welcome change from naans or chapattis

1 tbsp sunflower oil, for frying
2 large onions, chopped
1 large garlic clove, crushed
1 tsp ground cumin
1 tsp ground coriander
1 tsp grated peeled fresh root ginger
1/4 tsp ground cloves
1/2 tsp chilli powder
400ml hot vegetable stock (made with 1/2 stock cube and boiling water)
1 tsp caster sugar

3 potatoes, cut into large cubes
2 x 400g tins chickpeas, drained
2 x 200g bags Young leaf spinach by Sainsbury's, rinsed
4 tomatoes, cut into wedges
1 tbsp snipped chives, to garnish
3 tbsp low-fat natural yogurt, to serve

FOR THE BHATURA
85g wholemeal flour
85g plain flour, plus extra for dusting

1 tsp baking powder
1/4 tsp bicarbonate of soda
1/2 tsp caster sugar
3 tbsp low-fat natural yogurt
2 tbsp skimmed milk
100ml sunflower oil, for frying

1 Heat the oil in a pan, add the onions and stir-fry for 2 minutes. Add the garlic and all the spices and fry for 30 seconds.

2 Pour in the stock and stir in the remaining ingredients except the spinach and tomatoes and then season to taste. Bring to the boil, stir, partially cover and simmer for 15 minutes. Stir in the spinach until beginning to wilt, add the tomatoes, partially cover and cook for a further 5 minutes, until the spinach is tender and everything is bathed in a rich sauce. Taste and adjust the seasoning if necessary.

3 Meanwhile, make the bhatura. Mix all the ingredients together, using enough milk to form a soft, but not sticky, dough. Working quickly, knead the dough gently on a floured surface and shape into 6 balls. Roll out each to 10cm in diameter.

4 Heat the oil for deep-frying to 180°C, or until a cube of day-old bread becomes golden in 30 seconds. Slide a bhatura into the hot oil and fry for about 2 minutes, turning once, until puffy and golden. Remove from the pan with tongs or a fish slice, drain on kitchen paper and keep warm while cooking the remainder in the same way. Reheat the oil each time.

5 Spoon the chickpea masala into bowls. Top each with a spoonful of yogurt and sprinkle with the chives. Serve with the bhatura.

Per serving: 2104kJ/503kcal (25%), 21.8g fat (31%), 4.1g saturates (21%), 8.8g sugars (10%), 1.01g salt (17%)

SERVES 8
PREP 20 minutes,
plus chilling
COOK 45 minutes

Asparagus quiche

This light, fragrant quiche is ideal served warm and just set, with a slight wobble. Here spears of seasonal fresh asparagus are the focal point of a delicious dish

375g ready-rolled light shortcrust pastry by Sainsbury's

FOR THE FILLING
2 x 100g packs of asparagus spears by Sainsbury's
extra virgin olive oil
115g soft cheese light

2 tsp chopped thyme leaves
freshly ground black pepper
80g lighter mature cheese, grated
2 eggs
130ml half-fat crème fraîche

1 Preheat the oven to 200°C/180°C fan/gas 6. Remove the pastry from the fridge and unwrap it. Cut a circle a little larger than a 20cm loose-bottomed tart tin and line the tart tin with the pastry. Line the pastry case with greaseproof & non-stick baking paper by Sainsbury's and fill with baking beans.

2 Bake in a preheated oven for 10 minutes, then remove the paper and beans, and bake for a further 5 minutes. Remove from the oven and allow to cool. Reduce the oven temperature to 180°C/160°C fan/gas 4.

3 Toss the asparagus spears gently in a little olive oil. Cook on a hot griddle pan for 2 minutes on each side.

4 Spread the soft cheese over the pastry case. Sprinkle with the thyme, some pepper and the cheese. Trim the asparagus spears to fit, scatter the trimmings over the cheese and lay the spears on top.

5 Beat the eggs and crème fraîche together, seasoning to taste. Pour into the pastry case. Bake in the oven for about 30 minutes, until golden and just set. This quiche works equally well served warm or cold.

Per serving: 1241kJ/248kcal (15%), 18.1g fat (26%), 9.7g saturates (49%), 1.6g sugars (2%), 0.50g salt (8%)

SERVES 4
PREP 10 minutes
COOK 15 minutes

Mixed mushroom and pak choi stir-fry

This dish uses mushroom varieties that originate in Japan to accompany the Japanese soba noodle; though chestnut mushrooms make a great alternative. Use any leftover mushrooms the next day to make a half portion of the mushroom sauce on p296

250g dried soba or udon noodles
4 tbsp soy sauce reduced salt by Sainsbury's or tamari
1 tbsp lemon juice
2 tsp grated peeled fresh root ginger
2 garlic cloves, crushed
1 tsp chopped lemongrass, or lemongrass paste by Sainsbury's
1 tbsp caster sugar
¼ –½ tsp wasabi paste
225g frozen soya beans, defrosted

2 tbsp sunflower oil
a bunch of spring onions, trimmed and sliced
2 celery sticks, cut into matchsticks
100g shiitake mushrooms, sliced
100g oyster mushrooms, sliced
100g enoki mushrooms, trimmed of base and separated
2 heads pak choi (about 200g), coarsely shredded
2 tbsp sesame seeds, to garnish

1 Cook the noodles according to the pack instructions. Drain, cover and set aside.

2 Meanwhile, whisk the soy sauce, lemon juice, ginger, garlic, lemongrass, sugar and wasabi paste in a small bowl with 2 tablespoons of water, cover and set aside.

3 Boil the soya beans in water for 3 minutes. Drain, cover and set aside.

4 Heat the oil in a large frying pan or wok. Add the spring onions and celery and stir-fry for 2 minutes. Add all the mushrooms and stir-fry for 3 minutes. Add the pak choi and soya beans and stir-fry for 1 minute.

5 Add the noodles and the bowl of soy sauce mix. Toss until everything is heated through and coated. Spoon into bowls and sprinkle with sesame seeds before serving.

Per serving: 1857kJ/442kcal (22%), 13.5g fat (19%), 1.8g saturates (9%), 14.4g sugars (16%), 2.48g salt (41%)

Did you know?

Tamari is a Japanese form of soy sauce that is low in wheat or, sometimes, wheat free. It's traditionally made as a byproduct of miso paste. Tamari has a darker colour, richer flavour and less-salty taste, which makes it great for dipping too.

SERVES 8
PREP 20 minutes
COOK 25 minutes,
plus cooling

Bean Scotch eggs

A great veggie alternative to a popular picnic favourite - in fact, committed carnivores might well be converted

9 eggs
4 tablespoons olive oil
1 onion, finely chopped
3 x 410g tins cannellini beans by Sainsbury's, drained and rinsed
4 sundried tomatoes, drained and chopped

100g fresh white breadcrumbs
a handful of fresh parsley, chopped
plain flour, for dusting
100g dried breadcrumbs

1 Place 8 of the eggs into a pan of cold water. Bring to the boil and then cook for 8 minutes. Drain and cool under the cold tap. Then peel, cover and set aside.

2 Heat 1 tablespoon of the oil in a pan, add the onion and cook for 5 minutes, until soft. Leave to cool a little, then tip into a food processor with the beans and pulse until a coarse paste forms. Beat the other egg and stir into the mixture along with the sundried tomatoes, parsley and fresh white breadcrumbs. Season to taste.

3 Divide the bean mixture into 8 and use your hands to flatten each one out. Place onto a square of cling film. Dust flour all over an egg, place in the centre of the bean mixture and then use the cling film to help wrap the mixture around the egg, smoothing around the sides, until they are fully enclosed in the mixture. Repeat for the remaining eggs. Place the dried breadcrumbs on a plate and then roll the eggs in this, pressing a little so they are totally coated with the crumbs.

4 Heat half the remaining oil in a non-stick frying pan and cook half the eggs for about 7-10 minutes, turning often with a pair of tongs, until they're golden all over. Repeat for the remaining eggs. Then leave to cool. These beany eggs are delicious on their own or serve with tomato ketchup or brown sauce for dipping, if you prefer.

Per serving: 1366kJ/326kcal (16%), 12.9g fat (18%), 2.9g saturates (15%), 3.0g sugars (3%), 0.41g salt (7%)

Imam bayildi

Legend has it that this wonderful stuffed aubergine dish from Turkey is named after a priest who after eating it fainted with pleasure. Traditionally, the dish is prepared by placing the filling on top of the halved aubergines and pressing the filling down into them

4 small or medium, long, slim aubergines, stalks cut off
sunflower oil, for frying
150ml olive oil by Sainsbury's
juice of 1 lemon
2 tsp sugar
a small bunch of fresh flat-leaf parsley, chopped, to garnish

FOR THE FILLING
2 medium red onions, cut in half lengthways and finely sliced

4 garlic cloves, finely chopped
390g carton of chopped tomatoes by Sainsbury's
2 tsp sugar
1 tbsp olive oil
a bunch of fresh flat-leaf parsley, finely chopped
a bunch of fresh dill, finely chopped

1 Make the filling by placing the onions in a bowl with the garlic. Drain the tomatoes and add to the bowl. Then add the sugar and olive oil and mix well. Mix the parsley and dill into the onion mixture, season to taste, cover and set aside.

2 Partially peel the aubergines in thick stripes using a sharp knife or a vegetable peeler. Place in a bowl of salted water for 5 minutes, then rinse and pat dry with kitchen paper. In a pan, heat enough sunflower oil for frying and fry the aubergines over a medium heat, turning them over to make sure all the peeled areas turn golden. Fry until they soften and give when pressed with a finger.

3 Lift the aubergines onto kitchen paper to drain; then transfer to a chopping board. Carefully slit them open, end to end, keeping both ends and the base intact, so that the aubergines resemble canoes.

4 Spoon the onion and tomato mixture into the aubergine pockets, packing it tightly, until all the mixture is used. In a deep, heavy-based pan, place the aubergines side by side. In a bowl, mix the olive oil and lemon juice, pour over the aubergines and sprinkle over the sugar.

5 Cover the pan and place over a medium heat to create some steam. Reduce the heat and cook the aubergines gently for 45-50 minutes, basting occasionally, until they are soft and tender and only a little caramelised oil is left in the pan. Season to taste and leave to cool in the pan. Best served warm with a garnish of chopped parsley.

Per serving: 1348kJ/326kcal (16%), 30.6g fat (44%), 4.0g saturates (20%), 8.5g sugars (9%), <0.01g salt (<1%)

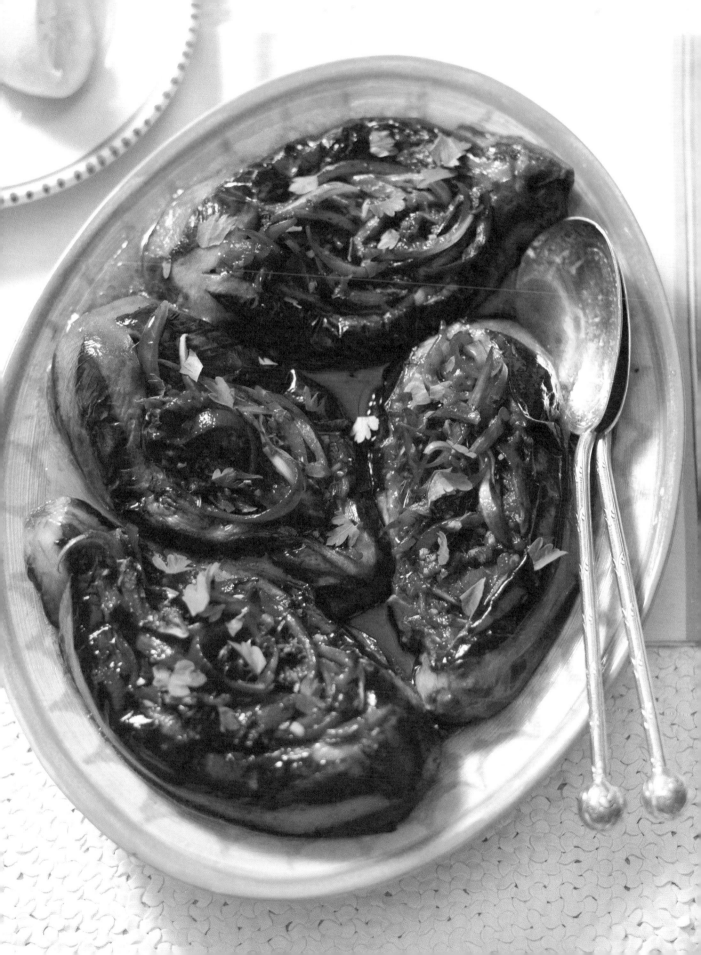

SERVES 6
PREP 25 minutes
COOK 1¼ hours

Vegetable casserole with dumplings

Dumplings add an extra dimension to this tasty casserole and can be made using a variety of different herbs

1 tbsp olive oil
1 onion, roughly chopped
3 garlic cloves, finely chopped
a pinch of dried chilli flakes
2 leeks, trimmed and
thickly sliced
3 carrots, peeled and
roughly chopped
2 celery sticks, roughly chopped

1 tbsp plain flour
900ml hot vegetable stock
(made with 1 stock cube and
boiling water)
410g tin haricot beans by
Sainsbury's, drained and rinsed
a few sprigs of fresh rosemary
crusty bread, to serve

FOR THE DUMPLINGS
225g self-raising flour
115g vegetable suet
2 tbsp finely chopped
flat-leaf parsley

1 Preheat the oven to 160°C/140°C fan/gas 3. Meanwhile, heat the oil in a large flameproof casserole over a medium heat, add the onion and cook for 3-4 minutes, until soft. Season to taste then stir through the garlic and chilli flakes. Add the leeks, carrots and celery and continue cooking for a further 10 minutes, stirring occasionally, until softened. Stir in the plain flour, then gradually stir in the hot stock. Add the haricot beans and rosemary. Bring to the boil, then reduce to a simmer, cover and put in the oven for 1 hour, checking on the liquid level as it cooks and topping up with hot stock if needed.

2 While this is cooking, prepare the dumplings. Mix together the flour, suet and parsley and season to taste. Add about 120ml cold water to form a soft, slightly sticky dough, trickling in more water if it seems too dry. Form into 12 balls and drop them into the stew for the last 30 minutes of cooking. Push them down so they are just immersed and cover with the lid.

3 Remove the lid for the last 10 minutes, or until the dumplings take on some colour. Remove the rosemary sprigs, ladle the casserole into warmed bowls. Serve with crusty bread.

Per serving: 1704kJ/407kcal (20%), 16.2g fat (23%), 7.1g saturates (36%), 12.1g sugars (13%), 1.04g salt (17%)

Cook's tip

If you like, you can cook this in a slow cooker. Preheat the slow cooker, if necessary. Follow step 1, using 600ml of stock, until the haricot beans and rosemary have been added. Then transfer everything to the slow cooker. Cover with the lid and cook on auto/low for 6–8 hours or on high for 4 hours. About 45 minutes before the end of the cooking time, prepare the dumplings as directed in step 2 and continue the recipe as above.

Pumpkin, spinach and dolcelatte lasagne

The fresh sage and savoury nutmeg bring the flavours alive in this rich lasagne. If pumpkin is out of season, use butternut squash or sweet potato instead

a small pumpkin or butternut squash (about 800g) peeled, halved, deseeded and chopped into bite-sized pieces
1 tbsp olive oil
8 fresh sage leaves, roughly chopped
a pinch of grated nutmeg

a pinch of dried chilli flakes (optional)
a pinch of allspice
200g bag of Young leaf spinach by Sainsbury's, rinsed
10 lasagne sheets by Sainsbury's
110g dolcelatte cheese, chopped

FOR THE SAUCE
60g Butterlicious spread by Sainsbury's
60g plain flour
900ml skimmed milk
1 bay leaf

1 Preheat the oven to 200°C/180°C fan/gas 6. Place the pumpkin in a large roasting tin, add the oil, season to taste and toss to coat; the tin must be large or the pumpkin will steam rather than roast. Sprinkle over the sage, nutmeg, chilli flakes, if using, and allspice and stir. Roast for 20-30 minutes, stirring halfway, until golden, then remove.

2 Stir in the spinach, which will wilt in a few minutes. Cover and set aside. Reduce the oven temperature to 190°C/170°C fan/gas 5.

3 For the sauce, melt the spread in a medium pan. Remove from the heat and blend in the flour. Gradually blend in the milk, stirring constantly with a wooden spoon or small wire whisk. Add the bay leaf. Return to the heat and bring to the boil, stirring all the time until thickened, then cook for 2 minutes, continuing to stir as before. Season to taste, discard the bay leaf, cover and set aside.

4 Spoon half the pumpkin and spinach into a 20cm x 30cm ovenproof dish. Seasoning to taste between each layer, add half the lasagne sheets, half the sauce and half the dolcelatte. Repeat to use up all the ingredients. Bake in a preheated oven for 30-40 minutes, until golden and bubbling. Delicious served with a lightly dressed green salad.

Per serving: 1764kJ/420kcal (35%), 15.8g fat (23%), 6.6g saturates (33%), 14.1g sugars (16%), 0.85g salt (14%)

Spinach and pine nut flatbread

This Valencian version of pizza – known as coca d'espinacs – is given a juicy topping of greens finished with a Middle Eastern sprinkling of pine nuts, raisins and olive oil

FOR THE BREAD BASE
100g strong bread flour
25g fresh yeast or
1 tsp dried yeast
1 tbsp olive oil,
plus extra for greasing

FOR THE TOPPING
500g spinach leaves
1-2 garlic cloves, slivered
1 tbsp pine nuts by
Sainsbury's, toasted
1 tbsp raisins or sultanas
olive oil, for drizzling

1 Sift the flour into a warm bowl. In a separate bowl, dissolve the yeast in 4 tablespoons of warm water, sprinkle with a little flour and leave for about 15 minutes to froth.

2 Make a well in the flour; then pour in the oil and the yeast mixture. Draw the flour into the liquid and knead the dough into a smooth ball. Place the dough in a bowl, cover with cling film and leave in a warm place for 1-2 hours, until doubled in size.

3 Preheat the oven to 220°C/200°C/gas 7. Wash the spinach, drain and cook it in a little water in a lidded pan. As soon as the leaves start to wilt, remove from the heat, squeeze dry and chop roughly. Cover and set aside.

4 Knead the dough well for 8-10 minutes to distribute the air bubbles and cut in half, then pat or roll each piece into a circle about 1cm thick. Transfer to a lightly oiled baking tray, top with the spinach, sprinkle with the garlic, pine nuts and raisins, drizzle with a little olive oil and leave for 10 minutes to prove.

5 Bake for 15-20 minutes, until the crust is puffy and blistered at the edges.

Per serving: 1808kJ/431kcal (22%), 15.7g fat (22%), 2.3g saturates (12%), 10.3g sugars (11%), 0.02g salt (<1%)

Did you know?
In its simplest and most traditional form, the coca is a flatbread, much like the Middle Eastern pitta, finished with a drizzle of olive oil. Slices of Serrano ham, cheese, chorizo and fried green peppers are traditionally served on the side.

SERVES 6
PREP 15 minutes
COOK 50 minutes

Middle Eastern lentils with chickpeas and peppers

Chickpeas have been used in many cuisines for thousands of years and are a typical Middle Eastern ingredient

100g brown or green
lentils, rinsed
1 tbsp olive oil
1 onion, finely chopped
3 garlic cloves, finely chopped
a pinch of dried oregano
finely grated zest and juice
of 1 lemon
½ tsp ground allspice
a pinch of grated nutmeg
½ tsp ground cumin

2 red peppers, deseeded and
sliced into strips
200g basmati rice
900ml hot vegetable stock
(made with 1 stock cube
and boiling water)
400g tin chickpeas by
Sainsbury's, drained and rinsed
a bunch of fresh parsley,
finely chopped

TO SERVE
150g low-fat natural yogurt
6 pitta breads

1 Put the lentils in a large heavy-based pan or tagine, season to taste and cover with water. Bring to the boil, then simmer for about 30 minutes, until they are beginning to soften, but don't let them turn mushy. Drain, cover and set aside.

2 Meanwhile, heat the oil in another heavy-based pan over a medium heat, add the onion and cook for 3-4 minutes, until soft. Season to taste then stir through the garlic, oregano, lemon zest, allspice, nutmeg and cumin and cook for a minute.

3 Add the peppers and cook for about 5 minutes, stirring to coat with spices. Cook for a further 2-3 minutes, until soft, then stir in the rice along with a little stock. Bring to the boil, add most of the stock and boil for a minute. Reduce to a simmer, add the chickpeas and cook on a very low heat for 15-20 minutes. Check occasionally that it's not drying out, topping up with a little hot stock if needed. Stir through the lentils, taste and season if necessary, then add the parsley and lemon juice. Serve with yogurt and pitta breads.

Per serving: 1817kJ/430kcal (22%), 6.7g fat (10%), 2.5g saturates (13%), 9.1g sugars (10%), 1.26g salt (21%)

Cook's tip

You can cook this dish in a slow cooker. At the beginning of step 2, preheat the cooker. Once you have brought everything to the boil in step 3, transfer the mixture to the slow cooker, add the chickpeas and just enough stock (about 600ml) to cover. Add the lid and cook on high for 1½–2 hours. About 5 minutes before the end of the cooking time, stir through the lentils, put the lid back on and let the lentils warm through. Taste and season as necessary, then add the chopped parsley and lemon juice.

Courgette, ricotta and mint tart

Capture the flavours of summertime with this mouth-watering tart to serve up to guests at an al-fresco lunch

plain flour, for dusting
500g shortcrust pastry block by Sainsbury's
2 courgettes, thinly sliced into long strips using a vegetable peeler
4 eggs, plus 1 egg yolk
150ml lighter crème fraîche by Sainsbury's

150ml semi-skimmed milk
finely grated zest of 1 lemon
a handful of fresh mint leaves, chopped
25g Basics Italian hard cheese by Sainsbury's, grated
50g ricotta cheese from Sainsbury's deli counter

1 Lightly flour your work surface, then roll out the pastry to a large 5mm-thick circle. Carefully place inside a 23cm deep tart tin with a removable bottom or a springform tin. Trim around the edge with a pair of scissors, leaving a 1cm collar to allow for the pastry to shrink a little. Then, chill in the fridge for at least 15 minutes. Meanwhile, preheat the oven to 200°C/180°C fan/gas 6.

2 Remove the tin from the fridge and line the pastry case with greaseproof and non-stick baking paper by Sainsbury's and fill with baking beans. Bake in a preheated oven for 10 minutes. Then remove the beans and paper and cook for a further 5-10 minutes until golden and crisp. Set aside to cool. Then, turn the oven down to 180°C/160°C fan/gas 4.

3 Sprinkle the courgette strips with a little salt, toss together and then place in a sieve set over the sink. Leave for 15 minutes. Then rinse and place inside a clean tea towel and squeeze really well to remove all the excess water.

4 Lightly beat the eggs together with the crème fraîche, milk, lemon zest, mint and most of the hard cheese. Season to taste.

5 Place the tart case on a baking sheet and carefully pour over the egg mixture. Separate the courgette strips and then arrange over the tart letting some rise out to give a bit of texture. Place little teaspoons of ricotta among the courgette and then sprinkle with the remaining Parmesan. Bake in a preheated oven for 30-35 minutes, until just set. Leave to cool for 10 minutes, or cool completely, then cut into slices and serve.

Per serving: 1723kJ/413kcal (21%), 26.7g fat (38%), 13.4g saturates (67%), 2.7g sugars (3%), 0.26g salt (4%)

Pumpkin and parsnip cassoulet

This vegetarian version of the traditional meat cassoulet features haricot beans and a crisp, herb breadcrumb and cheese topping

2 tbsp olive oil
1 onion, finely chopped
3 garlic cloves, finely chopped
2 carrots, peeled and finely chopped
2 celery sticks, finely chopped
1 bay leaf
450g pumpkin (prepared weight), chopped into bite-sized pieces (or use butternut squash)

450g small parsnips, peeled and sliced into rounds
250ml white wine
a few sprigs of fresh thyme
4 tomatoes, chopped, or use a 390g carton of chopped tomatoes by Sainsbury's
410g tin haricot beans, rinsed and drained

900ml hot vegetable stock (made with 1 stock cube and boiling water)

FOR THE TOPPING
125g fresh breadcrumbs, lightly toasted
30g Basics Italian hard cheese by Sainsbury's, grated
1 tbsp chopped flat-leaf parsley

1 Preheat the oven to 180°C/160°C fan/gas 4. Heat the oil in a large flameproof casserole over a medium heat, add the onion and cook for 3-4 minutes, until soft. Season to taste, add the garlic, carrots, celery and bay leaf, and cook, stirring occasionally, on a very low heat for 8-10 minutes, until all vegetables are soft.

2 Stir through the pumpkin and parsnip and cook for a few minutes more, then pour in the wine. Increase the heat, stir and let it bubble for a minute or two. Then add the thyme, tomatoes, beans and stock, and bring to the boil. Reduce to a simmer, season to taste, cover with the lid and put in the oven for 40 minutes.

3 Mix together the topping ingredients in a bowl, sprinkle it over the cassoulet, cover and put it back in the oven for 30 minutes. Then remove the lid and cook for about 10 minutes, until the topping is golden. Ladle into warmed bowls and serve.

Per serving: 1164kJ/277kcal (14%), 7.5g fat (11%), 2.1g saturates (11%), 14.2g sugars (16%), 1.11g salt (19%)

Cook's tip
If you like, you could make this dish in a slow cooker. Preheat the slow cooker at the beginning of step 1. Then, using a large heavy-based pan, follow step 1 to the point of adding the wine. Let the cassoulet bubble for a minute or two and then add the thyme, tomatoes and beans. Transfer everything to the slow cooker. Pour over 300ml of stock, season to taste and stir. Cover with the lid and cook on auto/low for 8 hours, or on high for 4 hours. An hour before the end of the cooking time, mix the topping ingredients together in a bowl, sprinkle over and replace the lid. Serve as above.

Crispy Provençal roll

A delicious filo pastry vegetable centrepiece for a summer feast

1 small aubergine, cut into
bite-sized pieces

2 courgettes, sliced

2 red peppers,
deseeded and sliced

3 tbsp olive oil

4 sheets ready-rolled filo
pastry by Sainsbury's

50g unsalted butter, melted

a handful of fresh basil
leaves, chopped

125g ball mozzarella cheese,
drained and torn into pieces

50g Basics Italian hard cheese
by Sainsbury's, grated

15g pine nuts

1 Preheat the oven to 200°C/180°C fan/gas 6.

2 Toss the aubergine, courgettes and peppers in 2 tablespoons of olive oil and place in a shallow roasting tray, making sure that they are spread out. Season to taste and then roast in a preheated oven for 25-30 minutes, until soft. Cover and set aside to cool.

3 Unroll the pastry onto a work surface. Lightly dampen some kitchen paper and place over the pastry to ensure it doesn't dry out. Mix together the remaining tablespoon of oil with the melted butter. Ease off one pastry sheet and lay out flat. Brush all over with the butter mixture. Then top with another piece of pastry and repeat.

4 Pile up half the vegetables in a line along the length of the pastry, leaving a 2.5cm border. Scatter over the basil and mozzarella and then top with the remaining vegetables and the Italian hard cheese. Fold over the ends of the pastry and then loosely roll up until the vegetables are fully enclosed.

5 Carefully place, seam-side-down, on a baking sheet and then brush over the top with more of the butter mixture. Scatter over the pine nuts and bake in the oven for 25 minutes, or until golden and crisp. Leave to cool for 5 minutes and then serve.

Per serving: 1167kJ/281kcal (14%), 20.6g fat (29%), 9.3g saturates (47%), 5.7g sugars (6%), 0.37g salt (6%)

SERVES 6
PREP 20-25 minutes,
plus chilling
COOK 40-45 minutes

Baked polenta with mixed mushrooms

This dish brings together the delicious combination of polenta and cheese with unusual mushrooms for a tasty meal

375g polenta by Sainsbury's
2 tbsp olive oil, plus extra for brushing
250g mixed mushrooms, for example portobello, chestnut and shiitake, trimmed and sliced
375g closed cup white mushrooms by Sainsbury's, quartered

3 garlic cloves, finely chopped
5-7 sprigs of fresh thyme or fresh rosemary, leaves picked
120ml dry white wine
250ml water
4 tbsp half-fat crème fraîche
250g mozzarella
fresh herbs or green salad leaves, to garnish

1 Sprinkle 2 oven trays with water. Bring 1.5 litres of water to the boil in a pan. Over a medium heat, slowly whisk in the polenta in a thin, steady stream. Cook, stirring, for 10-15 minutes, until thick enough to pull away from the pan, yet soft and smooth. Spread on the baking sheets in a layer about 30cm square. Cool, cover, then chill for 1 hour until firm.

2 Heat the oil in the frying pan. Add all the mushrooms, the garlic and herbs and cook, stirring, for 5-7 minutes, until the mushrooms are tender and the liquid has evaporated. Add the wine, simmer for 2-3 minutes, then add the water and cook until reduced by half. Pour in the crème fraîche, cook until the liquid thickens and season to taste.

3 Preheat the oven to 220°C/200°C fan/gas 7. Brush a 36cm x 23cm baking dish (or one with similar dimensions) with oil. Cut the chilled polenta into six 10cm squares and arrange half the squares in the dish in a single layer.

4 Spoon half the mushroom sauce over each square, then half the cheese. Repeat with another layer of polenta and mushrooms and top with the remaining cheese. Bake in a preheated oven for 20-25 minutes, until the cheese has melted.

5 Garnish with some fresh herbs or salad leaves and serve straightaway.

Per serving: 976kJ/234kcal (12%), 14.4g fat (21%), 7.4g saturates (37%), 1.8g sugars (2%), 0.40g salt (7%)

Pulses

Pulses are versatile and great store cupboard staples. These beans, lentils and peas are used from dried or from cooked and tinned in soups, stews, curries and salads in cuisines that span the globe

Puy lentils ^
These small, green lentils from France are particularly good braised with vegetables and also in salads. They have an earthy, rich flavour and hold their shape even after cooking.

> Cannellini beans
A member of the haricot family, these classic Tuscan white beans have a creamy, nutty flavour.

^ Yellow split peas
Dried split peas are a staple of Indian dhal and other vegetarian dishes, and in the traditional British dish of pease pudding.

^ Borlotti beans
Big, brown, rich, meaty and with a lovely creamy texture, these beans are excellent in pasta dishes, stews, soups and bakes as they hold their shape even when cooked for a long time.

< Haricot beans
Popular small, white beans, particularly used in cassoulets, and for baked beans in tomato sauce. They are excellent all-rounders for soups, casseroles and stews, with a mild flavour and a soft, creamy, yet slightly floury texture.

^ Red lentils
These small, split lentils cook quickly to a pulp. They are ideal for soups and sauces as they thicken the liquid naturally; they're essential for spicy dhals.

< Red kidney beans
These robust, floury-textured beans have a sweet, full bodied-flavour. They taste particularly good with chilli peppers and strong spices.

^ Butter beans
Large, soft and floury with a slightly dry texture when cooked, these beans have a distinctive, rich flavour. They are great for soups, stews, dips and pâtés.

^ Flageolet beans
These pretty green beans have an excellent, creamy texture and a mild sweet flavour. They are great in salads and take on flavours such as garlic and herbs well.

< Chickpeas
These coarse pulses have a distinctive, nutty flavour and a buttery texture. They hold their shape even after long cooking times. Purée cooked chickpeas for houmous, dips and sauces.

^ Soya beans
These silky-textured beans have a mild flavour, which makes them a good base for complex flavour combinations. Also used for making other soya products such as tofu.

^ Aduki beans
Richly coloured with a good, sweet, nutty flavour, they are excellent beans that hold their shape well. Great used in casseroles, soups and stews, and also good for burgers.

Warm new potato salad with caramelised red onions

With its sweet onions and sharp dressing, this salad works well with barbecued or grilled meats (see p100) or ribs (see p158)

1kg small new potatoes, halved lengthways

2 tbsp olive oil

2 red onions, finely sliced

2 tbsp balsamic vinegar

1 tsp light brown sugar

FOR THE DRESSING

4 tbsp extra virgin olive oil, plus extra if needed

2 tbsp red wine vinegar by Sainsbury's

2 tsp Dijon mustard

1 tsp caster sugar

1 Cook the potatoes in plenty of boiling water until just tender, 10-15 minutes depending on their size. Then drain well into a colander.

2 Meanwhile, heat the oil in a large, deep-sided frying pan. Cook the onions over a low heat for about 10 minutes, until they soften, then add the vinegar and sugar and cook for a further 10 minutes, until dark and glossy. Season to taste.

3 Whisk together the dressing ingredients in a salad bowl and season to taste. While the potatoes are still warm, but not too hot, toss them through the dressing. Lastly, add the red onions and they're ready to serve.

Per serving: 1011kJ/242kcal (12%), 11.2g fat (16%), 1.6g saturates (8%), 7.1g sugars (8%), 0.16g salt (3%)

Cook's tip
If the potatoes are not being served immediately, then wait to add the dressing until ready to eat as the potatoes often absorb the dressing as they cool.

SERVES 4
PREP 10 minutes
COOK 1 hour–1 hour
20 minutes

Oven-baked ratatouille

A classic ratatouille is a time-consuming dish to prepare. Here's a simple baked version for busier days

1 aubergine, cut into 3cm cubes
1 red pepper, deseeded and cut into 2.5cm cubes
1 yellow pepper, deseeded and cut into 2.5cm cubes
1 red onion, cut into 2.5cm cubes
1 courgette, cut into 2.5cm cubes

3 garlic cloves, roughly chopped
6 tbsp olive oil by Sainsbury's
335g cherry tomatoes by Sainsbury's
2 tbsp roughly chopped flat-leaf parsley leaves
1 tbsp thyme leaves

1 Preheat the oven to 200°C/180°C fan/gas 6.

2 In a bowl, mix together the aubergine, peppers, red onion, courgette and garlic. Toss them in 4 tablespoons of the oil and season to taste.

3 Spread them out into a single layer in 1 large or 2 smaller roasting tins. Drizzle with the remaining 2 tablespoons of oil and bake in a preheated oven for 40 minutes, until the vegetables are starting to colour at the edges. If you are using two oven shelves, switch the roasting tins over after 20 minutes, so that they both have a chance to cook near the top of the oven.

4 Take the vegetables out of the oven and scatter the cherry tomatoes and herbs over them. Gently mix them in, arranging the vegetables so that most of the tomatoes are on top, and cook for a further 20 minutes, until the tomatoes are starting to burst and the vegetables are cooked through.

Per serving: 919kJ/221kcal (11%), 16.3g fat (23%), 2.3g saturates (12%), 11.8g sugars (13%), 0.03g salt (<1%)

Cook's tip
Bake double or triple quantities of this dish and use the leftovers, with the addition of lasagne sheets and béchamel sauce (see p162), to make a delicious roasted vegetable lasagne.

Courgettes with garlic and mint

Sweet and juicy courgettes - cooked as here - make a great veggie accompaniment

2 tbsp olive oil by Sainsbury's
1 tbsp unsalted butter
400g small courgettes, sliced
into 1cm rounds

1 garlic clove, crushed
1 tbsp finely chopped mint

1 Melt the oil and butter in a large flameproof casserole or heavy-based saucepan with a lid; ideally, one that will fit the courgettes in a single layer.

2 Add the courgettes and stir them around so that as many as possible are touching the bottom of the pan. Cover and cook over a medium-high heat for 3 minutes.

3 Remove the lid, stir in the garlic and mint and season to taste. Re-cover and cook for a further 2 minutes, shaking occasionally, until the courgettes are just cooked and golden.

Per serving: 382kJ/93kcal (5%), 8.5g fat (12%), 2.7g saturates (14%), 1.7g sugars (2%), <0.01g salt (<1%)

Boulangère potatoes

Try these for a tasty accompaniment to roast and grilled meat
or fish or even a hearty stew

2 tbsp unsalted butter, plus
extra for greasing
1 tbsp olive oil
1 onion, finely sliced
1 garlic clove, crushed

900g waxy or yellow potatoes,
such as Charlotte, finely sliced
(using a food processor
or mandolin)

300ml hot vegetable stock
(made with $^1/_2$ stock cube and
boiling water)

1 Preheat the oven to 180°C/160°C fan/gas 4. Melt half the butter and the oil in a frying
pan and cook the onion over a medium heat for 5-7 minutes, until softened but without any
colour. Add the garlic and cook for another minute.

2 Rub the inside of a 20cm x 20cm deep-sided ovenproof dish with some butter. Spread
around half the potatoes. Arrange the onion and garlic over the potatoes, season to taste
and cover with the remaining potatoes. When you get to the top layer, arrange the potatoes
neatly. Pour over the stock and dot with the remaining butter.

3 Put the ovenproof dish on a large baking sheet and cook in the centre of the oven for
1 hour, or until the potatoes are soft and the top golden. Rest for 10 minutes before serving.

**Per serving: 721kJ/172kcal (9%), 6.8g fat (10%), 3.0g saturates (15%), 3.0g sugars
(3%), 0.38g salt (6%)**

Refried black beans with pico de gallo

Enjoy this Mexican-style side dish of mashed beans with a tomato salsa over rice for an enjoyable meat-free meal

450g dried black beans
by Sainsbury's
1 onion, roughly chopped
3 garlic cloves, roughly chopped
1 tsp olive oil

FOR THE PICO DE GALLO
2 tomatoes, diced
1 red onion, finely chopped
a handful of fresh
coriander, chopped
juice of 2 limes

TO SERVE
1 avocado, halved, stoned,
peeled and thinly sliced
30g lighter mature cheese by
Sainsbury's, grated (optional)

1 Put the dried beans, onion and garlic into a medium pan. Cover with water, season to taste and bring to the boil over a high heat. Reduce the heat and simmer, covered, for 2 hours, or until the beans turn soft. Drain the beans but reserve 250ml of the liquid.

2 Put the bean mixture along with the reserved liquid in a food processor, or use a hand blender, and blend until smooth.

3 In a heavy-based saucepan, heat the oil over a medium heat. Spoon the blended beans into the pan and cook, stirring frequently, for 5–6 minutes, or until thickened.

4 To make the pico de gallo, mix the tomatoes and onion with the coriander and lime juice. Serve the beans hot, topped with the pico de gallo and sliced avocado. If you like, add in some grated cheese and perhaps some soured cream.

Per serving: 878kJ/211kcal (11%), 12.0g fat (17%), 5.1g saturates (26%), 4.9g sugars (5%), 0.13g salt (2%)

Desserts

SERVES 6
PREP 20 minutes
COOK 10 minutes,
plus cooling

Raspberry tartlets

For a simple yet tasty alternative to a shortcrust pastry case,
try making these biscuit-based crusts instead

FOR THE BISCUIT CASE
200g Basics digestive
biscuits by Sainsbury's,
thoroughly crushed
50g caster sugar
75g Butterlicious spread by
Sainsbury's,
melted and cooled

FOR THE FILLING
100g caster sugar
40g cornflour
2 eggs
1 tsp Madagascan vanilla
extract by Sainsbury's
400ml semi-skimmed milk

225g raspberries
(about 6-7 large firm raspberries
per tartlet)
icing sugar, for dusting

1 Preheat the oven to 180°C/160°C fan/gas 4.

2 To make the base, in a bowl mix the biscuit crumbs, sugar and melted butter until
the mixture resembles wet sand.

3 Divide the biscuit mixture between six 12.5cm loose-bottomed tartlet tins or ramekins
and press it firmly into the bottom of each, allowing it to come up the sides as it spreads
out. Bake in a preheated oven for 10 minutes then set aside to cool. Once cooled, cover the
tart cases with cling film and store in the fridge until needed.

4 For the crème pâtissière, beat the sugar, cornflour, eggs and vanilla extract in a bowl.
In a heavy-based saucepan, bring the milk to the boil and take it off the heat just as it
bubbles. Pour the hot milk into the egg mixture, whisking all the time. Return the crème
to the pan and bring to the boil over a medium heat, whisking constantly. When the crème
thickens, reduce the heat to low and continue to cook for 2-3 minutes, whisking constantly.
Then transfer to a bowl, cover its surface with cling film (to prevent a skin forming) and
leave to cool completely.

5 Beat the cooled crème pâtissière well with a wooden spoon to make it ready to use.

6 When you are ready to assemble the tartlets, spoon or pipe the crème pâtissière into the
cases, top with raspberries and dust with icing sugar to serve.

Per serving: 1825kJ/435kcal (22%), 17.9g fat (26%), 7.1g saturates (36%),
39.2g sugars (44%), 0.73g salt (12%)

Get ahead
The tart cases can be chilled for up to
3 days and the crème pâtissière for up to 2 days if
well covered. You can also prepare the tart cases
in advance and keep them in the freezer for up to
2 months. You'll need to defrost thoroughly before
filling and serving as above.

SERVES 12
PREP 25 minutes
COOK 50-60 minutes,
plus cooling

Individual Black Forest pavlovas

This classic dessert is given a new twist with a moreish chocolate meringue base and clouds of whipped cream

4 egg whites
225g icing sugar, sifted
1 tsp cornflour
15g cocoa powder
1 tsp white wine vinegar
50g Belgian dark 76% cocoa cooking chocolate Taste the Difference, chopped

300ml whipping cream
8 tbsp morello cherry conserve by Sainsbury's
fresh cherries, pitted and halved, to serve

1 Line 2 oven trays with greaseproof paper & non-stick baking paper by Sainsbury's and preheat the oven to 140°C/120°C fan/gas 1.

2 Place the egg whites into a clean metal or glass bowl and whisk until stiff peaks form. Gradually whisk in 200g of the icing sugar, adding a tablespoon at a time, until the mixture is thick and glossy.

3 Carefully fold in the cornflour, cocoa powder, vinegar and chocolate until just combined.

4 Dollop 6 large spoonfuls of the mixture onto each oven tray and flatten slightly to make circles. Use a spoon to make a small dent in the centre of each and swirl around the edges to create a nice pattern.

5 Bake in a preheated oven for 50 minutes to 1 hour, until just crisp; check them regularly to ensure that they don't colour too much. Remove from the oven and leave to cool.

6 Lightly whip the cream with the remaining icing sugar. Mix 1 tablespoon of boiling water into the conserve if needed to loosen it. Spoon the cherry conserve over the centre of the meringues, then swirl over some cream and finish with some fresh cherries to share.

Per serving: 1178kJ/281kcal (14%), 12.1g fat (17%), 7.4g saturates (37%), 34.0g sugars (38%), 0.11g salt (2%)

Cook's tip
The undecorated meringues can be stored in an airtight container for up to 2 days.

Apple brown betty

A 'betty' is a baked fruit pudding topped with buttered breadcrumbs

85g unsalted butter

175g fresh breadcrumbs

900g Bramley apples

85g soft brown sugar

1 tsp ground cinnamon

½ tsp mixed spice

finely grated zest of 1 lemon

2 tbsp lemon juice

1 tsp Madagascan vanilla

extract by Sainsbury's

1 Preheat the oven to 180°C/160°C fan/gas 4. Then, melt the butter in a saucepan, add the breadcrumbs and mix well.

2 Peel, quarter and core the apples. Cut each quarter into slices and place in a bowl. Add the sugar, cinnamon, mixed spice, lemon zest and lemon juice and vanilla extract and mix well.

3 Put half the apple mixture into a 1.2-litre baking dish. Cover with half the breadcrumbs, then put in the rest of the apples and top with the remaining breadcrumbs.

4 Bake in a preheated oven for 35–45 minutes, checking after 35 minutes. If the top is colouring too much, reduce the temperature to 160°C/140°C fan/gas 3 and cover with greaseproof & non-stick baking paper by Sainsbury's. It is cooked when the crumbs are golden and the apples are soft. Serve immediately.

Per serving: 1313kJ/313kcal (16%), 12.5g fat (18%), 7.1g saturates (36%), 33.1g sugars (37%), 0.23g salt (4%)

Why not try?

A betty is simplicity itself to make, so this recipe lends itself well to all sorts of different fruits, though orchard fruits are best. Try changing the spices to suit your palate. Be creative: try lemon thyme with pears or star anise or cardamom with plums.

SERVES 8
PREP 40 minutes,
plus chilling
COOK 25 minutes,
plus cooling

Strawberry tart

This fresh fruit tart can easily be adapted by replacing the strawberries with other soft fruit

150g plain flour, plus extra
for dusting
100g unsalted butter,
chilled and diced
50g caster sugar
1 egg yolk

¹/₂ tsp Madagascan vanilla
extract by Sainsbury's
6 tbsp redcurrant jelly,
for glazing
300g strawberries, halved

FOR THE CRÈME PÂTISSIÈRE
100g caster sugar
40g cornflour
2 eggs
1 tsp Madagascan vanilla
extract by Sainsbury's
400ml semi-skimmed milk

1 In a bowl, rub the flour and butter together to form the consistency of fine breadcrumbs. Stir in the sugar. Beat together the egg yolk and vanilla extract, and add them to the flour mixture. Bring them together to form a dough; add a little water if it's dry. Wrap in cling film and chill for 1 hour. Preheat the oven to 180°C/160°C fan/gas 4.

2 Roll out the pastry on a lightly floured surface to a thickness of 3mm; if the pastry starts to crumble, bring it together with your hands and gently knead. Use the rolled-out pastry to line a 23cm loose-bottomed flan tin, leaving an overlapping edge of 2cm. Use a pair of scissors to trim any excess pastry and prick the base all over with a fork, to prevent air bubbles forming as it bakes.

3 Carefully line the pastry case with a piece of greaseproof & non-stick backing paper by Sainsbury's and scatter over baking beans. Place on an oven tray and bake for 20 minutes. Then, remove the beans and paper, and bake for a further 5 minutes. Remove from the oven and neaten the crust of any excess pastry.

4 Melt the redcurrant jelly with 1 tablespoon of water and brush a little over the pastry case. Set aside and leave to cool.

5 For the crème pâtissière, beat the sugar, cornflour, eggs and vanilla extract in a metal or glass bowl. In a heavy-based saucepan, bring the milk to the boil and take it off the heat just as it bubbles. Pour the hot milk into the egg mixture, whisking all the time. Return the crème to the pan and bring to the boil over a medium heat, whisking constantly. When the crème thickens, reduce the heat to low and continue to cook for 2–3 minutes, whisking constantly. Then transfer to a bowl, cover its surface with cling film (to prevent a skin forming) and leave to cool completely.

6 Beat the cooled crème pâtissière well with a wooden spoon to make it ready to use. Then, spread it over the pastry case and top with the strawberries. Reheat the jelly glaze and brush over the strawberries, then leave to set.

7 Once it's set, remove from the tin and serve. This tart is best eaten on the same day but will keep, covered, in the fridge overnight.

Per serving: 1522kJ/362kcal (18%), 13.4g fat (19%), 7.3g saturates (37%), 23.7g sugars (26%), 0.14g salt (2%)

Lemon meringue roulade

The traditional lemon meringue pie filling is given a new twist in this impressive dessert

5 egg whites,
at room temperature
225g caster sugar
1/2 tsp white wine vinegar
1 tsp cornflour
1/2 tsp Madagascan vanilla
extract by Sainsbury's

150g quark Be good to yourself
100g half-fat crème fraîche
100g lemon curd Taste the
Difference
icing sugar, for dusting

1 Preheat the oven to 180°C/160°C fan/gas 4 and line a 25cm x 35cm Swiss roll tin with greaseproof & non-stick baking paper by Sainsbury's.

2 Whisk the egg whites with an electric whisk on high speed, until stiff peaks form. Reduce the speed and whisk in the sugar, a little at a time, until thick and glossy.

3 Fold in the vinegar, cornflour and vanilla extract, trying to keep the mixture well aerated. Spread the mixture into the tin and bake in the centre of the oven for 15 minutes. Remove the meringue from the oven and allow to cool to room temperature.

4 Meanwhile, whip the quark and crème fraîche until thick but not stiff. Fold in the lemon curd until just blended; a few ripples will enhance the appearance of the roulade.

5 Sprinkle icing sugar over a fresh sheet of greaseproof & non-stick baking paper. Carefully turn the cooled roulade out of the tin onto the sugared paper and peel off the layer of paper that lined the tin. Spread the lemon cream over the roulade with a palette knife. Use the paper to roll up the meringue firmly but without squeezing out the cream.

6 Transfer the roulade so that it sits seam-side-down on a serving plate, then cover and chill until ready to serve. Before serving, lightly dust with icing sugar.

Per serving: 892kJ/211kcal (11%), 4.5g fat (6%), 2.9g saturates (15%), 36.8g sugars (41%), 0.23g salt (4%)

Meringue kisses

These little meringue kisses can be made with a choice of three delicious fillings or just one (each recipe makes 20)

FOR THE VANILLA MERINGUE
2 egg whites at room temperature
125g caster sugar
½ tsp Madagascan vanilla extract by Sainsbury's

FOR THE RASPBERRY RIPPLE FILLING
100ml whipping cream
1 tbsp caster sugar
100g raspberries

1 First make the vanilla meringue. Preheat the oven to 120°C/100°C fan/gas ½ and line 2 oven trays with greaseproof & non-stick baking paper by Sainsbury's.

2 Put the egg whites in a large clean bowl and whisk until the meringue holds soft peaks. Add the sugar, a spoonful at a time, whisking well after each addition. Continue whisking until the whites are stiff and glossy. Fold in the vanilla extract.

3 Fill a piping bag with the meringue and pipe 40 rosettes, 2.5cm apart onto the prepared trays. Bake until crisp and dry, about 1 hour. Cool completely before removing from the tray.

4 Now, make the raspberry filling. Whip the cream until it holds soft peaks then whisk in the caster sugar. Crush the raspberries with a fork and gently fold into the cream until 'rippled'.

5 Assemble the meringue kisses. Hold a meringue by its pointed end and scoop up a little of the filling on its flat underside; repeat with another meringue. Sandwich 2 prepared meringues together. Repeat with the remaining meringues. Refrigerate for 30 minutes to set the cream and serve chilled.

Per 'kiss': 210kJ/50kcal (3%), 2.0g fat (3%), 1.2g saturates (6%), 7.3g sugars (8%), 0.02g salt (<1%)

Why not try?

Here are two other great filling options to use for step 5 above.

Double chocolate filling

Whip 100ml whipping cream until it holds soft peaks then whisk in 1 tbsp caster sugar. Dip the underside of each meringue in 100g dark chocolate, melted and cooled, before sandwiching with the cream. Dust with 2 tsp cocoa powder.

Per 'kiss': 327kJ/78kcal (4%), 4.4g fat (6%), 2.7g saturates (14%), 8.4g sugars (9%), 0.02g salt (<1%)

Luscious lemon filling

whip 100ml whipping cream until it holds soft peaks then whisk in 1 tbsp caster sugar. Fold 4 tbsp lemon curd Taste the Difference into the whipped cream. Dust with icing sugar.

Per 'kiss': 291kJ/69kcal (4%), 3.0g fat (4%), 1.9g saturates (10%), 10.1g sugars (11%), 0.05g salt (<1%)

Banana frozen dessert

This simple frozen dessert is quick to create and a handy way to use up ripening or slightly over-ripe bananas

4 ripe bananas
1 tsp Madagascan vanilla
extract by Sainsbury's

1 Simply peel the bananas, chop them into 2cm chunks and put them in a container suitable for freezing. Seal and put in the freezer until frozen.

2 When the bananas are frozen solid, process them in a food processor with the vanilla extract until you have a thick creamy mixture. You may need to scrape down the sides a couple of times during the process.

3 Either eat the softened banana dessert immediately or freeze for a few minutes to firm it up once more before serving.

Per serving: 453kJ/107kcal (5%), <0.5g fat (<1%), 0.1g saturates (<1%), 20.9g sugars (23%), <0.01g salt (<1%)

Why not try?
Add a few spoonfuls of chocolate and hazelnut spread or smooth peanut butter in step 2 for a tasty variation to this dessert.

Blackberry fool

An elegant finale to a late summer meal, this fragrant dessert shows fresh blackberries at their best

1 tbsp sunflower oil by Sainsbury's

4 tbsp rosewater

1 tbsp powdered gelatine

350g blackberries

1 tbsp lemon juice

85g icing sugar, sifted

150ml low-fat Greek-style yogurt

300ml reduced-fat thick cream

4 egg whites

1 Wrap double-layered bands of greaseproof and non-stick baking paper by Sainsbury's around the outsides of 4 ramekins so they sit 5cm above the rim. Secure with adhesive tape. Brush the inside rim of the paper lightly with oil.

2 Place the rosewater in a small bowl, sprinkle with the gelatine, and leave to soak for 2 minutes, or until it becomes spongy. Set the bowl in a larger bowl, half filled with boiling water, and stir to dissolve the gelatine. Remove from the heat and allow to cool slightly.

3 Place all but 4 of the blackberries in a food processor and blend to a purée. Sieve, discarding any pips before stirring in the lemon juice and sugar, then stir in the gelatine. Leave in a cool place until just beginning to set.

4 Whip the yogurt and cream to soft peaks and fold into the blackberry mixture. In a separate bowl, whisk the egg whites until stiff and fold into the blackberry mixture. Pour into the ramekins, cover and chill in the fridge until set.

5 Remove from the fridge, peel off the greaseproof paper from each ramekin and decorate with the reserved whole blackberries.

Per serving: 1259kJ/301kcal (15%), 12.5g fat (18%), 6.6g saturates (33%), 32.6g sugars (36%), 0.24g salt (4%)

Why not try?
Make this recipe using any other soft berries or even a mixture of several.

SERVES 8
PREP 10 minutes
COOK 35 minutes, plus
cooling and chilling

Muhallabia

This Middle Eastern milk pudding, enhanced with the traditional notes of floral waters of the Orient, is delectable and moreish

60g fine rice flour
1 litre semi-skimmed milk
125g granulated sugar
2-3 tbsp rosewater

2 tbsp icing sugar, for dusting
a handful of pistachio kernels
by Sainsbury's finely chopped,
for sprinkling

1 In a small bowl, combine the rice flour with a little milk to form a loose paste. Pour the remaining milk into a heavy-based pan and stir in the sugar. Bring the milk to the boil, stirring constantly, until the sugar has dissolved.

2 Reduce the heat and stir a spoonful or 2 of the hot milk into the rice flour paste, then tip the mixture into the pan. Whisk the mixture well to prevent the flour from forming lumps. Bring the milk to the boil again and stir in the rosewater.

3 Reduce the heat to low and simmer for 20 minutes, stirring, until the mixture is thick enough to coat the back of the spoon.

4 Pour the mixture into a serving bowl, or individual bowls, and leave to cool, allowing a skin to form on top. Transfer to the fridge and chill. Just before serving, dust the tops with icing sugar and sprinkle over some chopped pistachios.

Per serving: 735kJ/174kcal (9%), 3.3g fat (5%), 1.4g saturates (7%), 24.7g sugars (27%), 0.20g salt (3%)

Why not try?
Decorate the dish with fresh rose petals for an elegant touch for a special occasion.

Strawberry semifreddo

Enjoy eating the classic summer combination of strawberries
and cream any time as a frozen dessert

vegetable oil, for greasing

225g strawberries, hulled, plus
extra whole strawberries and
redcurrants, to decorate

250ml double cream

50g icing sugar

124g meringue nests by
Sainsbury's, coarsely crushed

3 tbsp Crème de Cassis or
raspberry-flavoured liqueur

FOR THE COULIS

225g strawberries, hulled

30-50g icing sugar

1-2 tsp lemon juice

1 Lightly brush a 23cm loose-bottomed springform tin with vegetable oil, then line the base
with greaseproof and non-stick baking paper by Sainsbury's and set aside.

2 Purée the strawberries in a blender or food processor. Whip the cream with the icing
sugar until it just holds its shape. Fold the strawberry purée and cream together, then fold
in the crushed meringues and liqueur. Turn the mixture into the tin, smooth the surface,
cover with cling film and freeze for at least 6 hours, or overnight.

3 Next, make the strawberry coulis. Purée the strawberries in a blender or food processor,
then press them through a sieve to remove the seeds. Stir the icing sugar into the purée.
Flavour the coulis with lemon juice or your choice of brandy, grappa or balsamic vinegar.

4 Just before serving, remove the semifreddo from the tin, peel away the lining paper and,
using a warmed knife, cut into slices. Arrange the slices on individual plates, spoon the
coulis around the base, and decorate with whole strawberries and redcurrants.

Per serving: 1119kJ/268kcal (13%), 15.3g fat (22%), 9.3g saturates (47%), 30.1g sugars
(33%), 0.04g salt (<1%)

Cook's tip

This semifreddo can be stored in the freezer for up
to 3 months. If you like, use any of the following for
the lemon juice: brandy, grappa or balsamic vinegar.

SERVES 12
PREP 30 minutes
COOK 1 hour,
plus cooling

White chocolate and Irish cream cheesecake

This luxurious cheesecake combines rich, creamy white chocolate with a decadent hint of Irish cream liqueur

50g unsalted butter
150g Basics digestive biscuits by Sainsbury's, thoroughly crushed
200g white chocolate, broken into pieces

300ml half-fat crème fraîche
400g quark Be good to yourself by Sainsbury's
4 eggs
4 tbsp caster sugar

4 tbsp Irish cream liqueur by Sainsbury's
white chocolate curls (see Cook's tip), to decorate

1 Preheat the oven to 150°C/130°C fan/gas 2. Melt the butter in a small pan then stir together with the crushed biscuits until you have the consistency of wet sand.

2 Press the biscuit mixture into an 18cm springform tin and smooth over the top with the back of a spoon. Bake in the oven for 10 minutes, until crisp then leave to cool.

3 Place the chocolate and 100ml of the crème fraîche into a heatproof bowl. Set the bowl over a pan of simmering water, ensuring that that the bottom doesn't touch the water. Leave until the chocolate is melted, stirring occasionally, remove from the pan and cool a little.

4 Beat the quark for a minute until it is super-smooth. Gradually beat in the eggs and 2 tablespoons each of the caster sugar and Irish cream liqueur, until mixed through. Stir through the white chocolate mixture and pour into the cake tin.

5 Bake in a preheated oven for 45-50 minutes, or until there is just a slight wobble at the centre of the cake. Remove from the oven and run a sharp knife around the perimeter of the tin. Allow to cool before removing from the tin. Cover and place in the fridge for at least 3 hours or, preferably, overnight.

6 Whip the remaining crème fraîche with the remaining 2 tablespoons of caster sugar and Irish cream liqueur until soft peaks form. Swirl all over the cooled cake. Top with the white chocolate curls to serve.

Per serving: 1474kJ/353kcal (18%), 21.8g fat (31%), 12.8g saturates (64%), 23.6g sugars (26%), 0.41g salt (7%)

Cook's tip
To make white chocolate curls, melt 100g white chocolate in a heatproof bowl set over simmering water as above. Pour over a baking tray and leave to set. Angle the flat blade of a knife at about 45° to the chocolate, holding both the handle and the tip, and pull towards you gently to create curls. Lift the larger ones with a skewer to avoid finger marks. For finer curls, try using a zester.

Boston cream trifle

This rich dessert draws inspiration from the famous Boston cream pie, with its luscious layers of sponge and creamy custard

225g plain flour
2 tsp baking powder
115g unsalted butter, softened, plus extra for greasing
175g caster sugar
2 eggs, at room temperature
1 tsp Madagascan vanilla extract by Sainsbury's
120ml semi-skimmed milk

600g berries, such as blackberries, strawberries (hulled and halved), raspberries and blueberries
500g custard Be good to yourself

FOR THE GANACHE
350g dark chocolate, broken into small pieces
250ml double cream

1 Preheat the oven to 180°C/160°C fan/gas 4. Double sift the flour and baking powder into a bowl, cover and set aside. Using an electric hand whisk, cream together the butter and sugar in a separate bowl until light and fluffy. Add the eggs one at a time, whisking between additions, then add the vanilla extract. Fold in the flour mixture one-third at a time, alternating with the milk. Continue to fold until the mixture is smooth and everything is well incorporated.

2 Grease and line a 23cm square cake tin and pour in the mixture. Bake for 25 minutes, or until golden brown and springy to the touch. Remove from the oven and leave to cool.

3 For the ganache, heat the chocolate and cream in a small heatproof bowl over a pan of simmering water, ensuring that the bowl does not touch the water. Stir occasionally until the chocolate melts. Remove from the heat and set aside.

4 Slice the cake into ten 12cm squares and place a layer of cake at the bottom of a tall glass bowl. Spread some of the berries evenly on top of the cake, reserving a handful for decorating. Pour the custard over the berries and top with the remaining cake. Pour the ganache over the top and smooth out. Top with the remaining berries, cover and place in the fridge to chill. Serve chilled.

Per serving: 2265kJ/543kcal (27%), 29.0g fat (41%), 17.4g saturates (87%), 38.1g sugars (42%), 0.25g salt (4%)

Blueberry cheesecake

The marbled effect on this cheesecake is really simple to achieve,
but always looks impressive

50g unsalted butter, plus extra
for greasing
125g Basics digestive biscuits by
Sainsbury's, thoroughly crushed
150g blueberries
185g caster sugar
400g lighter soft cheese by
Sainsbury's

250g tub lighter Italian
mascarpone by Sainsbury's
2 large eggs, plus 1 large
egg yolk
1 tsp vanilla extract
2 tbsp plain flour, sifted

FOR THE COMPÔTE
100g blueberries
1 tbsp caster sugar
a squeeze of lemon juice

1 Preheat the oven to 180°C/160°C fan/gas 4. Grease the base and sides of a deep 23cm
springform cake tin. Melt the butter in a saucepan set over a low heat; don't let it turn brown.

2 Add the biscuit crumbs to the pan and stir until they are coated in butter. Remove from
the heat. Press the crumbs into the base of the tin using the back of a spoon.

3 Put the blueberries along with 3 tablespoons of the sugar in a food processor and whizz
until smooth. Push the mixture through a nylon sieve (metal will taint it) into a small pan.
Boil and then simmer for 3–5 minutes, or until thickened and jammy. Cover and set aside.

4 Place the remaining sugar and last five cheesecake ingredients in the rinsed-out food
processor. Whizz the mixture until smooth and very well combined. Pour the mixture onto
the biscuit base and smooth the top with a palette knife. Drizzle over the berry 'jam' and
make swirls in it by drawing a metal skewer deeply through the mix.

5 Wrap the sides of the cake tin with foil and put it into a deep roasting tray. Boil a kettle
of water and pour boiling water into the tray until it comes halfway up the sides of the cake
tin (this prevents cracking). Bake for 40–50 minutes, until the filling has just set. Cover with
greaseproof & non-stick baking paper by Sainsbury's if the top is colouring too much.

6 Remove from the oven and leave to cool for 10 minutes. Slide a palette knife round the
outside of the cheesecake to ease it from the tin, then leave in the tin to cool completely.
Once cool, remove the cheesecake from the tin and transfer to a serving dish.

7 Meanwhile, put all the ingredients for the compôte in a small pan. Heat gently, stirring
occasionally, until all the sugar dissolves. Then transfer to a jug to serve.

Per serving: 1252kJ/299kcal (15%), 15.6g fat (22%), 8.5g saturates (43%), 24.0g
sugars (27%), 0.37g salt (6%)

Why not try?
Change the fruits for the ripple for an alternative
taste and different coloured ripple effect.

SERVES 8
PREP 15-20 minutes
COOK 20-30 minutes

Key lime pie

This pie takes its name from the small limes that grow in the Florida Keys; this twist on the traditional pie uses a ginger biscuit base

75g unsalted butter
200g Basics ginger snaps by Sainsbury's or Freefrom digestive biscuits by Sainsbury's (for a gluten-free pie), crushed
5 limes

3 large egg yolks
397g tin sweetened condensed milk by Sainsbury's
pouring cream, to serve (optional)

1 Preheat the oven to 180°C/160°C fan/gas 4. Melt the butter in a saucepan over a low heat. Add the biscuit crumbs and stir until well combined. Remove from the heat and tip the mixture into a 23cm loose-bottomed flan tin, then use a spoon to press it evenly and firmly all over the base and sides of the tin. Place on an oven tray and bake for 5-10 minutes.

2 Meanwhile, finely grate the zest of 3 of the limes into a bowl. You can use a zester to pare long strands of zest from a fourth lime to decorate. Juice all 5 limes and set aside.

3 Place the egg yolks into the bowl with the lime zest, and whisk with an electric whisk until the egg has thickened. Pour in the condensed milk and continue whisking for another 5 minutes. Add the lime juice and whisk again until it is incorporated. Pour the mixture into the flan tin and bake for 15-20 minutes, or until set but still with a wobble in the centre.

4 Remove the pie from the oven and leave it to cool completely. Serve the pie decorated with the fine strands of lime zest, if you like, and accompanied by pouring cream, if using. The pie will keep in an airtight container in the fridge for a couple of days.

Per serving: 1555kJ/370kcal (19%), 17.8g fat (25%), 9.8g saturates (49%), 35.3g sugars (39%), 0.37g salt (6%)

Did you know?

A common baking mistake with deep-filled sweet tarts is to overcook them. So, be sure to remove them from the oven when they still have a slight wobble to them in the centre. They will cool and set to a creamy texture. Overcooking will result in a tart with an unpleasantly 'rubbery' texture.

Raspberry and hazelnut crème brûlée

This delicate take on the traditional brûlée looks impressive. The ground hazelnuts enhance the flavour of the raspberries beautifully

115g raspberries
140g caster sugar
1 tsp finely grated lemon zest
300ml reduced-fat thick cream
100ml half-fat crème fraîche

2 eggs
50g ground hazelnuts by Sainsbury's
$\frac{1}{2}$ tsp Madagascan vanilla extract by Sainsbury's

1 Divide the raspberries between each of the ramekins. Sprinkle with 1 tablespoon of the sugar followed by the lemon zest.

2 Whisk the cream with the créme fraîche, eggs, hazelnuts, vanilla extract and 1 tablespoon of the sugar. Pour over the raspberries. Stand the dishes in a large frying pan with enough boiling water to come halfway up the sides of the dishes. Cover the pan with a lid or foil and cook very gently for about 30 minutes, or until set. Don't let the water boil or the custard will curdle. Cover and leave to cool, then chill in the fridge.

3 Preheat the grill to its hottest setting. Remove the ramekins from the fridge, sprinkle liberally with the remaining sugar and grill for 3-4 minutes until caramelised. Alternatively, move a cook's blow torch back and forth across the surface to caramelise the sugar. Leave to stand for 5 minutes, then serve.

Per serving: 1742kJ/417kcal (21%), 22.5g fat (32%), 9.6g saturates (48%), 40.6g sugars (45%), 0.16g salt (3%)

SERVES 8
PREP 25 minutes,
plus chilling
COOK 30-35 minutes,
plus cooling

Pastel de Santiago

This lemony almond cake from Spain is baked in a light, crisp pastry shell. The top is traditionally decorated with a cut-out of St James's cross - the pilgrim's emblem

FOR THE PASTRY
100g Basics lard by Sainsbury's
100g caster sugar
1 egg yolk
200g plain flour,
plus extra for dusting
1 tsp ground cinnamon
icing sugar, for dusting

FOR THE FILLING
4 eggs
250g caster sugar
250g ground almonds
finely grated zest and
juice of 1/2 lemon

1 For the pastry, beat the lard with the sugar until light and fluffy. Beat in the egg yolk, sprinkle in a little flour and the cinnamon, then work in the remaining flour until you have a slightly soft ball of dough. Wrap in cling film and chill for 30 minutes, until firm.

2 Preheat the oven to 200°C/180°C fan/gas 6. On a lightly floured surface, roll out the pastry thinly using a floured rolling pin. Line a deep 23cm round flan tin with the pastry. Prick the base with a fork, cover with greaseproof & non-stick baking paper by Sainsbury's and weigh down with baking beans.

3 Bake blind for 8-10 minutes to set the pastry. Then, remove the baking paper and bake for a further 1-2 minutes. Remove from the oven and set aside to cool.

4 For the filling, whisk the eggs until light and fluffy. Sprinkle in the sugar, a spoonful at a time, and continue to beat until doubled in volume. Gently fold in the almonds and lemon zest and juice without overworking the mix and collapsing the air bubbles.

5 Spoon the mixture into the pastry case, filling it almost to the top, leaving a little edge of pastry. Bake for 20-25 minutes, until the topping is well-risen, firm and golden. Leave to cool before taking out of the tin. Dust with icing sugar before serving.

Per serving: 2627kJ/628kcal (31%), 33.3g fat (48%), 7.9g saturates (40%), 46.6g sugars (52%), 0.10g salt (2%)

Did you know?
The tart is named as a mark of respect for St James the apostle, whose sanctuary at Santiago de Compostela ranks with Rome and Jerusalem as a destination for pilgrims. The lemon in the filling is for the sorrow of Good Friday and the almonds serve as a reminder of the Holy Land.

Cakes
and bakes

SERVES 10
PREP 20 minutes
COOK 35 minutes,
plus cooling

Angel food cake with blackberry sauce

This show-stopping sponge cake, made without the addition of butter or oil, is as light as air

250g caster sugar
1 tsp salt
100g super-fine flour or
twice-sifted plain flour
12 large egg whites, at
room temperature
2 tsp Madagascan vanilla extract
by Sainsbury's

whipped cream, to
serve (optional)

FOR THE SAUCE
350g blackberries
3 tbsp runny honey
juice of 1 lemon

1 Heat the oven to 180°C/160°C fan/gas 4. In a food processor, process the sugar and salt until very fine. Sift the flour and half the sugar mixture into a bowl, cover and set aside.

2 Put the egg whites in another bowl and add the vanilla extract. Using an electric hand whisk or mixer, whisk for 5 minutes, or until the egg whites are stiff. Add the remaining sugar mixture, a little at a time, and keep beating so that the mixture remains stiff.

3 Fold the flour and sugar mix into the egg white mixture with a rubber spatula. When well incorporated, spoon the mixture into a non-greased 25cm Bundt tin or a ring mould with a capacity of 2.5 litres, and bake for 35 minutes. Leave the cake to cool for 1 hour in the tin.

4 Meanwhile, put the blackberries, honey and lemon juice in a non-reactive saucepan (not aluminium or cast-iron) and cook over a low heat. Simmer, stirring constantly, until the blackberries break down. Cover and set aside to cool.

5 To serve, turn the tin upside down and leave to cool; don't rush this step, as otherwise it can be tricky to remove the cake from the tin. Then, carefully turn the cake out onto a plate. Spoon over the blackberry sauce and serve with freshly whipped cream, if you like.

Per serving: 1267kJ/301kcal (15%), 10.6g fat (15%), 4.6g saturates (23%), 32.0g sugars (36%), 0.77g salt (13%)

Cook's tip
This recipe uses a lot of egg whites. Apart from making lots of omelettes or enriching custard sauces, why not use the leftover egg yolks in some home-made mayonnaise (see p162)?

SERVES 8
PREP 25 minutes
COOK 45-50 minutes

Chocolate and brazil nut cake

This unusual, rich and flourless cake uses Brazil nuts instead of the more usual almonds

75g unsalted butter, cubed, plus extra for greasing
100g Belgian dark 76% cocoa cooking chocolate Taste the Difference, broken into pieces
150g Brazil nuts
125g caster sugar

4 large eggs, separated
cocoa powder or icing sugar, to serve
extra-thick double cream, to serve (optional)

1 Preheat the oven to 180°C/160°C fan/gas 4. Grease a 20cm round springform cake tin and line the base with greaseproof & non-stick baking paper by Sainsbury's.

2 Melt the chocolate in a heatproof bowl over a pan of simmering water making sure the bowl doesn't touch the water, cover and leave to cool.

3 In a food processor, grind the nuts and sugar finely. Add the butter and pulse until just blended (see box below). Continue to blend while adding the egg yolks one at a time. Add the melted chocolate and blend.

4 In a separate bowl, whisk the egg whites to stiff peaks. Turn the chocolate mixture into a large bowl and beat in a few tablespoons of the egg whites to loosen it a little. Now carefully fold in the remaining egg whites with a large metal spoon.

5 Scrape the mixture into the tin and bake for 45-50 minutes, until the surface is springy and a skewer inserted into the middle comes out clean. Leave to cool in the tin for a few minutes then turn out on to a wire rack to cool completely.

6 Remove the baking paper and dust over the cocoa powder or icing sugar, whichever you prefer. If you like an indulgent dessert, then serve with a dollop of extra-thick cream.

Per serving: 1906kJ/460kcal (23%), 36.3g fat (52%), 16.2g saturates (31%), 20.4g sugars (23%), 0.12g salt (2%)

Cook's tip
Take care to pulse the butter into the nut and sugar mixture in short bursts, as prolonged processing will result in the natural oils in the nuts being released, which would give the finished cake an oily flavour.

SERVES 10
PREP 30 minutes
COOK 30–40 minutes,
plus cooling

Triple-layered coconut cake

There is something very indulgent about a triple-layered cake, and this one is no exception

225g unsalted butter, softened, plus extra
for greasing
400g caster sugar
115g coconut oil
2 tsp Madagascan vanilla extract by Sainsbury's
4 eggs, at room temperature
4 egg whites, at room temperature
550g plain flour, plus extra for dusting
½ tsp salt

1 tbsp baking powder
375ml coconut milk light by Sainsbury's
10g fresh coconut pieces by Sainsbury's, shredded,
to decorate

FOR THE VANILLA CREAM
500ml double cream
50g caster sugar
1 tsp vanilla extract

1 Preheat the oven to 180°C/160°C fan/gas 4. Using an electric hand whisk or a mixer, cream together the butter, sugar and oil. Beat in the vanilla extract, and then the eggs, one at a time. Once the eggs are fully incorporated, beat in the egg whites until light and fluffy.

2 Sift together the flour, salt and baking powder into a bowl. Add to the egg mixture, one-third at a time, alternating with the coconut milk. Beat together until fully incorporated and the mixture is light and fluffy.

3 Grease three 20cm round cake tins and lightly dust them with flour. Divide the cake mixture evenly between the tins. Bake for 30 minutes, two on the top shelf and one underneath, or until a skewer inserted into the centre comes out clean; the cake on the lower shelf will require an extra 10 minutes or so to cook through. Leave the cakes to cool for 10 minutes in the tin before transferring to a wire rack to cool completely.

4 Toss the shredded coconut in a frying pan over a medium heat until toasted.

5 For the vanilla cream, whip the cream, sugar and vanilla extract until stiff.

6 To assemble the cake, place one cake on a serving plate and spread one-third of the vanilla cream over it. Place the second cake over the cream and spread another one-third of the cream. Then top with the third cake and spread over the remaining cream. Sprinkle with the toasted coconut and serve.

Per serving: 3943kJ/946kcal (47%), 59.6g fat (85%), 39.1g saturates (196%), 48.8g sugars (54%), 0.91g salt (15%)

Top baking tips

1 Use tried-and-tested recipes and resist the temptation to make additions or substitutions – extra baking powder will make the cake rise quickly but then sink, and many low-fat spreads are not for baking.

2 Read the recipe through completely first and then follow step by step to avoid missing something out.

3 Weigh and measure ingredients accurately. Invest in good scales and use proper measuring spoons rather than cutlery.

4 When making cakes, use eggs and fats at room temperature to mix more easily.

5 Line cake tins carefully with greaseproof & non-stick baking paper by Sainsbury's or grease them and dust with flour.

6 Once wet and dry ingredients are combined, the raising agent starts to work immediately, so keep mixing and put the cake in the oven as soon as it is ready.

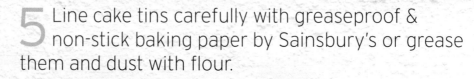

7 Always preheat the oven to the correct temperature to assist the cake in rising and use the middle shelf for an even bake.

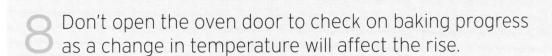

8 Don't open the oven door to check on baking progress as a change in temperature will affect the rise.

9 Stick to the cooking times in the recipe, but as ovens can vary, check the bake a little before the end of the cooking time. The spring in the cake should feel the same at the edges as in the middle, and the cake should slightly come away from the sides of the tin.

10 A skewer inserted into the cake should come out clean when the cake is ready. If not and the top is colouring as well, quickly put a piece of dampened greaseproof on top and bake for 5 minutes more and recheck.

11 Sponge cakes can be turned out on a rack to cool after a few minutes cooling in the tin; rich fruit cakes turn out better when they are left to cool completely in the tin.

12 Wait until a cake is thoroughly cooled before decorating.

13 Always use an airtight tin for storage. For baking ahead, sponge cakes can be frozen once cooled and kept undecorated and wrapped for up to 3 months.

MAKES 1 large or 2 smaller salami (serves 12)
PREP 15-20 minutes plus chilling

Rocky road salami

The popular no-bake chocolate bar gets a grown-up makeover, becoming a sweet treat that's perfect with coffee

250g Belgian dark 76% cocoa cooking chocolate Taste the Difference, broken into squares
150g unsalted butter, plus extra for the tin
2 tbsp golden syrup

200g rich tea biscuits by Sainsbury's, crushed
50g raisins
50g dried cranberries
100g mini marshmallows

1 Melt the chocolate, butter and syrup in a heatproof bowl over a pan of simmering water, making sure the bowl doesn't touch the water. When it has melted, allow to cool slightly.

2 Tip the biscuit crumbs into the chocolate mixture, followed by the dried fruit and lastly the marshmallows.

3 Put 3 overlapping layers of cling film on a work surface. To make smaller salami, place half the rocky road mix in a rough line a third of the way up from the bottom. Then roll the shorter piece over the mix, pulling it towards you through the cling film to make it compact. Roll it on the work surface to form a sausage shape, compressing the mixture tighter and tighter. Securely fasten the ends of the cling film and place in the fridge for at least 4 hours, or overnight, to set. Repeat with the remaining half of the mixture. To serve, remove from the fridge and slice into rounds using a sharp knife. If you prefer a larger salami, then just do this with all the mixture in one go.

Per serving: 1502kJ/361kcal (18%), 23.0g fat (33%), 13.8g saturates (69%), 22.5g sugars (25%), 0.20g salt (3%)

Why not try?
Use milk chocolate if you prefer, or a mix of dark and milk chocolate, to make this treat less rich. Mix up the flavours with other dried fruits, such as cherries and blueberries, and other biscuits, such as malted milk or digestives. Find your ultimate combination.

Cinnamon apple cake

This bake is equally delicious served warm as a dessert with a dollop of crème fraîche or simply cold with a cup of coffee

115g unsalted butter, cut into cubes, plus extra for greasing
200g plain flour, sifted, plus extra for dusting
3–4 Bramley apples, peeled, cored, quartered and sliced
1 tbsp lemon juice

3 eggs
250g caster sugar
6 tbsp semi-skimmed milk
4 tbsp single cream
1 tbsp baking powder
2 tsp ground cinnamon by Sainsbury's

1 Preheat the oven to 200°C/180°C fan/gas 6, and grease a 24cm square cake tin with butter and dust with flour.

2 Put the apple slices in a bowl of water with the lemon juice to prevent them browning.

3 In a large bowl, whisk the eggs and 225g of the sugar until thick and pale and the whisk leaves a trail when lifted out of the mixture.

4 Put the butter, milk and cream in a pan and melt gently, then bring to the boil. Leave to cool briefly, then stir into the egg mixture. Fold in the flour and baking powder. Pour the cake mixture into the prepared cake tin.

5 Drain the apples and arrange over the cake mixture. Mix the remaining sugar with the cinnamon and sprinkle over the top. Bake for 25–30 minutes, until golden. Remove from the oven, leave to cool in the tin then cut into squares to serve.

Per serving: 1121kJ/267kcal (13%), 10.4g fat (15%), 5.8g saturates (29%), 26.2g sugars (29%), 0.09g salt (2%)

Why not try?
Make this cake with pitted cherries, plums or apricots for other flavour combinations.

MAKES 24
PREP 20 minutes
COOK 10-15 minutes

Pistachio and cranberry cookies

These cookies have contrasting colours but perfectly complementary tastes

100g unsalted butter, softened
200g soft light brown sugar
1 egg, lightly beaten
1 tsp vanilla extract
1 tbsp runny honey by Sainsbury's
125g self-raising flour, sifted

125g porridge oats
100g pistachio nuts, lightly toasted and roughly chopped
100g dried cranberries, roughly chopped
a little semi-skimmed milk, if needed

1 Preheat the oven to 190°C/170°C fan/gas 5, and line 2 or 3 oven trays with greaseproof and non-stick baking paper by Sainsbury's.

2 Put the butter and sugar in a bowl and cream together with a hand-held electric whisk until smooth. Add the egg, vanilla extract and honey and beat well.

3 Add the flour and oats, stirring with a wooden spoon to combine. Add the chopped nuts and cranberries, and mix until thoroughly combined. If the mixture is too stiff, add a little milk until it becomes pliable.

4 Take walnut-sized pieces of the cookie dough and roll them into balls between your palms. Place on the prepared oven trays and flatten slightly, spacing them well apart on the trays.

5 Bake in a preheated oven for 10-15 minutes, until golden (you may need to do this in batches). Leave on the tray to cool and transfer to a wire rack. These wonderfully chewy cookies will keep in an airtight container for up to 5 days.

Per serving: 616kJ/147kcal (7%), 6.2g fat (9%), 2.5g saturates (13%), 12.6g sugars (14%), 0.05g salt (<1%)

Why not try?
Once you have mastered this recipe for oat cookies, try experimenting with different combinations of fresh or dried fruit and nuts, or adding seeds such as sunflower seeds and pumpkin seeds into the cookie dough mixture.

MAKES 9
PREP 40 minutes,
plus rising and cooling
COOK 30 minutes

Pecan caramel cinnamon buns

Sweet, sticky, and oozing with home-made caramel, these cinnamon buns are perfect for a sumptuous weekend brunch

FOR THE DOUGH
7g sachet fast action dried yeast by Sainsbury's
100g caster sugar
125ml semi-skimmed milk
115g unsalted butter
a pinch of salt
1 egg
550g plain flour, plus extra for dusting
vegetable oil, for greasing

FOR THE CARAMEL SAUCE
200g light soft brown sugar
115g Butterlicious spread by Sainsbury's
1 tsp vanilla extract
125ml single cream

FOR THE FILLING
90g Butterlicious spread by Sainsbury's
85g light soft brown sugar

1 tbsp ground cinnamon
125g pecans, chopped

FOR THE ICING
125g icing sugar
1 tbsp semi-skimmed milk

1 In a bowl, dissolve the yeast in 60ml warm water with a pinch of the sugar. Set aside for 5-7 minutes, or until it begins to bubble. In a pan, heat the milk and butter over a low heat until the butter has melted. Remove immediately from the heat. In a medium bowl, mix the yeast mixture, the remaining sugar, salt, egg, the melted butter mixture and half the flour. Stir to mix, then add the remaining flour, until the mixture comes together to form a dough.

2 Knead the dough for 5 minutes, adding flour as necessary so that it is not tacky. Transfer it to an oiled bowl, cover with cling film and keep in a warm place for 1 hour, until well risen.

3 Meanwhile, make the caramel sauce. In a heavy-based frying pan, melt the sugar, stirring constantly with a whisk. The sugar will clump, but continue to stir. Once the sugar has melted and darkened, add the butter. Continue to stir as the butter melts and incorporates. Add the vanilla extract and cream, and continue stirring until the boiling has stopped. Remove from the heat and leave to cool.

4 Preheat the oven to 180°C/160°C fan/gas 4. Turn out the dough onto a floured surface and roll it out to a thickness of 1cm. To make the filling, melt the butter and mix with the sugar, cinnamon and pecans. Spread the filling over the dough and roll up into a tight spiral.

5 Pour the caramel sauce into a 23cm square baking tin. Cut the dough roll into 9 equal slices and press into the caramel sauce. Bake for 25-30 minutes, or until the buns are golden and the caramel is bubbling. The centre of the buns should remain slightly gooey. Whisk together the icing sugar and milk. Pour the icing over the hot buns. Serve straightaway.

Per serving: 3310kJ/790kcal (40%), 35.3g fat (50%), 9.1g saturates (46%), 60.1g sugars (67%), 0.71g salt (12%)

MAKES 1 loaf
PREP 25 minutes, plus
overnight fermenting,
rising and proving
COOK 40-50 minutes

Artisan rye bread

Breads made with rye flour are a popular tradition in Central
and Eastern Europe. This version uses a starter dough instead
of using yeast for the bread's airiness

FOR THE STARTER
150g rye flour
150g live natural yogurt
1 tsp fast action dried yeast
by Sainsbury's
1 tbsp black treacle
1 tsp caraway seeds, lightly
crushed

FOR THE DOUGH
150g rye flour
200g strong white bread flour,
plus extra for dusting
1 tsp salt
vegetable oil, for greasing
1 egg, beaten, for glazing
1 tsp caraway seeds, to decorate

1 In a bowl, mix all the starter ingredients together with 250ml tepid water. Cover and leave
overnight. When you look at it the next day, it should be bubbling.

2 For the dough, mix the flours together with the salt and stir into the starter. Mix to make
a dough, adding a little extra water if required. Turn out onto a floured surface and knead
for 5-10 minutes, or until smooth and springy. Shape into a ball, transfer to an oiled bowl
and cover loosely with cling film. Leave in a warm place for 1 hour, or until doubled in size.

3 Dust flour on to an oven tray. Lightly knead the dough again and form it into a rugby-ball
shape. Lift onto the tray, re-cover it loosely and leave to prove for another 30 minutes.

4 Preheat the oven to 220°C/200°C fan/gas 7. Brush the dough with the beaten egg and
immediately sprinkle it evenly with the caraway seeds. Slash the loaf along its length.

5 Bake for 20 minutes, then reduce the temperature to 200°C/180°C fan/gas 6. Bake for
a further 20-30 minutes, until dark golden. Cool on a wire rack.

Per serving: 711kJ/168kcal (8%), 1.6g fat (2%), 0.6g saturates (3%), 2.2g sugars (2%),
0.46g salt (8%)

Why not try?
Make a seeded rye bread by kneading in 100g mixed
seeds, such as pumpkin, sunflower, sesame, poppy
seeds and pine nuts, in step 3.

MAKES 1 loaf
PREP 20 minutes,
plus rising and proving
COOK 40-45 minutes

A classic white loaf

Mastering a classic white loaf should be a starting point for all amateur bakers. Nothing beats the taste of fresh, crusty white bread, still warm from the oven

500g very strong white bread flour, plus extra for dusting
1 tsp fine salt
2 tsp fast action dried yeast by Sainsbury's

1 tbsp sunflower oil by Sainsbury's, plus extra for greasing

1 Put the flour and salt into a bowl. In a small bowl, dissolve the dried yeast in 300ml warm water. Once it has dissolved, add the oil. Make a well in the centre of the flour. Pour in the liquid, stirring to form a rough dough. Use your hands to bring the dough together.

2 Turn the dough out onto a lightly floured work surface. Knead for 10 minutes until smooth, glossy and elastic. Put the dough in a lightly oiled bowl, cover loosely with cling film and leave to rise in a warm place for up to 2 hours, until doubled in size.

3 When the dough has risen, turn it out onto a floured surface and knock it back to its original size. Knead it and shape it into the desired shape; a long, curved oblong shape will produce a bloomer. Place the dough on an oven tray, cover it with cling film and a tea towel, and leave it in a warm place until well risen and doubled in size. This could take 30 minutes to 1 hour. The bread is ready to bake when it is tight and well risen, and a finger poked into the dough leaves a dent that springs back quickly.

4 Preheat the oven to 220°C/200°C fan/gas 7. Place one oven shelf in the middle of the oven, and one below it, close to the bottom of the oven. Boil a kettle full of water. Now slash the top of the loaf 2 or 3 times with a knife on the diagonal. This will allow the bread to continue to rise in the oven. Dust the top with flour and place it on the middle shelf. Place a roasting pan on the bottom shelf of the oven and then quickly pour the boiling water into it and shut the door - the steam created in the oven will help the bread to rise.

5 Bake the bread for 10 minutes, then reduce the oven temperature to 190°C/170°C fan/gas 5 and bake it for 30-35 minutes, until the crust is golden and the bottom sounds hollow when tapped. Reduce to 180°C/160°C fan/gas 4 if it is starting to colour too quickly. Remove the bread from the oven and leave to cool on a wire rack.

Per serving: 645kJ/152kcal (8%), 1.4g fat (2%), 0.2g saturates (1%), 0.6g sugars (4%), 0.41g salt (7%)

SERVES 8
PREP 30-35 minutes,
plus rising and proving
COOK 15-20 minutes

Rosemary focaccia

This Italian flatbread is incredibly versatile and responds well to whatever flavours you want to experiment with

1 tbsp fast action dried yeast by Sainsbury's
425g strong white bread flour, plus extra for dusting
2 tsp salt
leaves from 5-7 sprigs of fresh rosemary, two-thirds finely chopped

½ tsp freshly ground black pepper
90ml olive oil, plus extra for greasing

1 Sprinkle the yeast over 4 tablespoons of warm water in a bowl. Leave for 5 minutes, stirring once. In a large bowl, mix the flour with the salt and make a well in the centre. Add the chopped rosemary, 4 tablespoons of oil, yeast, pepper and 240ml lukewarm water.

2 Gradually draw in the flour and work it into the other ingredients to form a soft and sticky dough. Do not be tempted to add more flour to dry it out. Sprinkle the dough with flour and knead for 5-7 minutes on a floured work surface. When ready, the dough will be very smooth and elastic.

3 Place in an oiled bowl and cover with a damp tea towel. Leave to rise in a warm place for 1-1½ hours, until doubled in size. Put the dough on a floured work surface and knock out the air. Cover with a dry tea towel and leave to rest for 5 minutes.

4 Brush an oven tray with oil. Transfer the dough to the tray and flatten the dough with your hands so it is evenly filled.

5 Cover with a tea towel and leave to prove in a warm place for 35-45 minutes, until puffed.

6 Preheat the oven to 200°C/180°C fan/gas 6. Scatter the reserved rosemary leaves on top. With your fingertips, poke the dough all over to make deep dimples.

7 Pour spoonfuls of the remaining oil all over the dough. Bake on the top shelf for 15-20 minutes, until browned. Transfer to a wire rack to cool.

Per serving: 1214kJ/289kcal (15%), 12.2g fat (17%), 1.8g saturates (9%), 0.8g sugars (<1%), 0.62g salt (10%)

Cook's tip
This focaccia dough can be left in the fridge to rise overnight. You'll just need to bring it back to room temperature before baking.

SERVES 8
PREP 10-15 minutes
COOK 25-35 minutes

Southern US-style cornbread

This quick American cornbread is traditionally served as an accompaniment for a barbecue, soup or stew; it would work perfectly with some pulled pork (see p170)

50g unsalted butter, melted and cooled, plus extra for greasing
250g fine cornmeal or polenta
2 tsp baking powder

¹/₂ tsp fine salt
2 large eggs
250ml buttermilk by Sainsbury's
1 tbsp runny honey (optional)

1 Preheat the oven to 220°C/200°C fan/gas 7. Grease a 19cm loose-bottomed round cake tin or similar-sized flameproof cast-iron frying pan and place it in the oven to heat up.

2 In a bowl, mix the cornmeal, baking powder and salt. Whisk together the eggs and buttermilk. Make a well in the centre of the cornmeal mixture and pour in the buttermilk mixture, stirring. Stir in the melted butter and honey, if using, and mix.

3 Remove the hot cake tin or frying pan from the oven and pour in the mixture. The tin or pan should be hot enough to make the batter sizzle as it goes in, this is what gives the cornbread its distinctive crust.

4 Bake in the middle of the oven for 20-25 minutes, until it has risen and is colouring at the edges. Leave to cool for 5 minutes before turning out and slicing as a side dish.

Per serving: 515kJ/123kcal (6%), 6.9g fat (10%), 3.6g saturates (18%), 5.7g sugars (6%), 0.48g salt (8%)

Why not try?
Make a spicier version by adding 1 red chilli, deseeded and finely chopped, and 4 tbsp finely chopped coriander at the same time as the honey.

SERVES 4 (makes 12)
PREP 15 minutes
COOK 15 minutes,
plus cooling

Buttermilk biscuits with a creamy mushroom sauce

A favourite dish of the American South where they call these scone-like bakes 'biscuits'. These versatile bakes can work with a sweet or a savoury accompaniment. Try them with a rich sauce for a tasty snack

FOR THE BISCUITS
250g self-raising flour, plus extra for dusting
1 tsp baking powder
½ tsp fine salt
100g unsalted butter, softened
100ml buttermilk by Sainsbury's, plus extra for brushing
1 tbsp runny honey

FOR THE SAUCE
2 tbsp olive oil
15g unsalted butter
250g chestnut mushrooms, sliced
200ml chicken stock (made with ½ stock cube and boiling water)
100ml dry white wine
2 sprigs of fresh thyme, leaves picked
4 tbsp lighter crème fraîche by Sainsbury's

1 Preheat the oven to 200°C/180°C fan/gas 6. Sift the flour and baking powder into a bowl and add the salt. With your fingertips, rub the butter into the dry ingredients until the mixture resembles fine crumbs.

2 Make a well in the centre and pour in the buttermilk and honey. Work the mixture together to form a rough dough, then turn it out onto a lightly floured work surface and bring it together into a smooth ball. Do not overhandle it or the biscuits may harden.

3 Roll out the dough to a thickness of 2cm and use a 6cm cutter to stamp out rounds. Gather up the remaining dough, re-roll and cut out more rounds until all the dough is used.

4 Place the dough circles on a non-stick oven tray and brush the tops with buttermilk, to give them a golden finish. Bake in the oven for 15 minutes, until golden and well risen.

5 Meanwhile, heat the oil and butter in a large, non-stick frying pan. Add the mushrooms to the pan, stir well and cook over a medium heat for 5 minutes, stirring, until the juices have evaporated. Add the stock, wine and thyme. Season to taste, bring to the boil and cook for 5 minutes to reduce the sauce. Stir in the crème fraîche and heat through.

6 Once the biscuits are cooked, remove them from the oven and cool for 5 minutes on a wire rack before serving, still warm, with the mushroom sauce alongside. If necessary, the biscuits can be kept in an airtight container for 1 day and warmed up again in the oven.

Per serving: 2324kJ/557kcal (28%), 32.6g fat (47%), 16.9g saturates (85%), 8.8g sugars (10%), 1.78g salt (30%)

Sainsbury's food safety advice

General kitchen safety guidelines

● Wash your hands thoroughly before food preparation. If handling raw meat, fish or poultry, it's equally important to wash your hands after preparation, too.

● Keep raw food separate from ready-to-eat foods when you're preparing meals; use separate chopping boards and utensils or wash thoroughly between use.

● Washing raw chicken spreads bacteria around the kitchen via tiny splashes, which increases the risk of cross-contamination to other foods. The best way to destroy harmful bacteria is by cooking thoroughly, until piping hot throughout with no pink colour remaining in the flesh.

● Refer to ingredient packaging for full preparation and cooking instructions.

● Public health advice is to avoid eating raw or lightly cooked eggs, especially for those vulnerable to infections, including pregnant women, babies and the elderly.

● Wash fresh vegetables, fruit and herbs (including any used for garnishing dishes) before use.

● When reheating leftovers, make sure they are piping hot throughout.

Freezing and defrosting

● Products can be frozen up to the use-by date (check labels to see if suitable for freezing).

● Defrost food overnight in the fridge (covered in a dish to avoid contaminating other products).

Refrigerating food

● Keep your fridge temperature below 5°C.

● To avoid cross-contamination, cover raw meat and poultry and store at the bottom of the fridge, separate from ready-to-eat food.

● When preparing food, keep out of the fridge for the shortest time possible.

● Cool down leftovers as quickly as possible then, once cooled, transfer them to the fridge and eat within 2 days.

● Clean your fridge regularly to ensure it remains hygienic and in good working condition.

● For tinned food, decant the contents into a non-metallic container.

'Best before' and 'use-by' dates

● Food with a 'best before' date is longer-lasting. It is safe to eat after this date but will not be at its best quality.

● Food with a 'use-by' date goes off quite quickly and what's more it could pose a health risk if consumed after this date.

Recipe nutrition

The nutritional information on each recipe shown in this book has been calculated using Sainsbury's own-brand products and is based on 1 adult portion, assuming equal division of the recipe into the suggested number of servings.

Nutrition is calculated using each recipe's ingredients list only and does not include any sides, accompaniments or other serving suggestions mentioned in the method. The nutrition content will vary if other products are used or if the servings are not identical. Also, variations in cooking methods may affect the nutritional content.

The nutritional information on each recipe also includes the percentage of Reference Intakes (RIs) provided by a serving. RIs are a guide to the maximum amounts of calories, fat, saturates, sugars and salt an adult should consume in a day (based on an average female adult) and are as on the right.

Seasoning: we're committed to promoting healthier eating and lowering salt in daily diets. As such we have worked hard to produce recipes that do not need as much (if any) salt seasoning. Note: recipe nutrition does not include any salt you add yourself.

Energy or nutrient	Reference intake per day
Energy	8400kJ/2000kcal
Total fat	70g
Saturates	20g
Total sugars	90g
Salt	6g

For more information on food safety and nutrition, visit sainsburys.co.uk/livewellforless and sainsburys.co.uk/kitchensafety

Index

303

Credits

LONDON, NEW YORK, MELBOURNE, MUNICH, AND DELHI

DK UK

Senior Editor Nikki Sims
Project Art Editor Katherine Raj
Project Editor Cressida Tuson
Managing Editor Dawn Henderson
Managing Art Editor Christine Keilty
Senior Jacket Creative Nicola Powling
Editorial Assistants Claire Gell,
Alice Kewellhampton
Design Assistant Laura Buscemi
Senior Pre-Production Producer Andy Hilliard
Senior Producer Verity Powell
Creative Technical Support Sonia Charbonnier
Art Director Peter Luff
Publisher Peggy Vance
Art Director and Food Stylist Kat Mead
Prop Stylist Liz Haraala-Hamilton
Photography Max Hamilton

DK India

Art Editors Gazal Bawa, Vikas Sachdeva
Assistant Art Editor Gursimran Singh
Managing Art Editor Navidita Thapa
Pre-Production Manager Sunil Sharma
DTP Designer Satish Chandra-Gaur

For Sainsbury's

Book team Phil Carroll, Mavis Sarfo,
Lynne de Lacy, Tony Jagpal
Nutrition Alastair McArthur
Product safety manager Nikki Mosley

Special thanks to

Seven Publishing for nutritional calculations
on the recipes.

Printed and bound by
Leo Paper Products Limited, China.

ISBN-13: 978-0-2411881-2-5

All the forest sources in this product have
been risk assessed for legality and responsible
management. To find out more about our values
and best practices go to **www.dk.com**

Conversion chart

Weights

Metric	Imperial	Metric	Imperial
15g	1/2oz	300g	11oz
25g	1oz	350g	12oz
40g	1 1/2oz	375g	13oz
50g	2oz	400g	14oz
60g	2 1/2oz	425g	15oz
75g	3oz	450g	1lb
100g	3 1/2oz	500g	1lb 2oz
125g	4oz	650g	1lb 7oz
150g	5oz	675g	1 1/2lb
175g	6oz	700g	1lb 9oz
200g	7oz	750g	1lb 11oz
225g	8oz	900g	2lb
250g	9oz	1kg	2lb 4oz
275g	10oz	1.5kg	3lb 6oz

Volumes

Metric	Imperial	Metric	Imperial
25ml	1fl oz	350ml	13fl oz
50ml	2fl oz	400ml	14fl oz
75ml	3fl oz	450ml	16fl oz (3/4 pint)
100ml	4fl oz	600ml	20fl oz (1 pint)
150ml	5fl oz (1/4 pint)	750ml	25fl oz (1 1/4 pints)
175ml	6fl oz	900ml	30fl oz (1 1/2 pints)
200ml	7fl oz	1 litre	34fl oz (1 3/4 pints)
225ml	8fl oz	1.2 litres	40fl oz (2 pints)
250ml	9fl oz	1.5 litres	52fl oz (2 1/2 pints)
300ml	10fl oz (1/2 pint)	1.8 litres	60fl oz (3 pints)